John Proffatt

The Curiosities and Law of Wills

John Proffatt

The Curiosities and Law of Wills

ISBN/EAN: 9783744667166

Printed in Europe, USA, Canada, Australia, Japan

Cover: Foto ©Suzi / pixelio.de

More available books at **www.hansebooks.com**

THE CURIOSITIES

AND

LAW OF WILLS.

BY

JOHN PROFFATT, LL.B.,

Counsellor-at-law, author of "Woman before the Law."

"Wills, and the construction of them, do more perplex a man than any other matter; and to make a certain construction of them exceedeth *jurisprudentum artem.*"—COKE.

SAN FRANCISCO:
SUMNER WHITNEY & Co.
1876.

TABLE OF CONTENTS.

Introduction 9

CHAPTER I.

Origin and History of Wills 29

CHAPTER II.

Form and Requisites of Wills 41
    Section 1. Nuncupative Wills.
              2. Written Wills.

CHAPTER III.

Testamentary Capacity 68
    Section 1. Incapacity as to Age.
              2. Physical or Mental Incapacity.
              3. Senile Dementia.
              4. Coverture.

CHAPTER IV.

Legacies 93
    Section 1. As to their Quality.
              2. Legacies Vested or Contingent.
              3. Conditional Legacies.
              4. Payment of Legacies.
              5. The Person who may take.

CHAPTER V
LIMITS TO TESTAMENTARY DISPOSITION. ... 130

CHAPTER VI.
REVOCATION OF WILLS.................. 152

CHAPTER VII.
WILLS AS AFFECTED BY DOMICILE......... 173

CHAPTER VIII.
CONSTRUCTION OF WILLS............. ... 185

PREFACE.

It is far from the thoughts of the publishers or the author of this book to provide a work merely for entertainment; it is hoped the title will not mislead so as to suggest this idea.

While it is sought to make it entertaining and the style animated, in the selection of such apt and striking cases as will illustrate and expound the principles and rules of law relating to wills, the main idea has been to make it useful and reliable as a systematic, clear, and concise summary for the student and lawyer, and interesting to all classes of readers.

It is not expected that it will be used as a work of reference on the various subjects connected with wills; but it is hoped it will be found so accurate and practical as to make it serve advantageously for a manual on this subject, so that a careful reading of it will give a correct knowledge of the law relating to this interesting and important subject.

It could not be expected that, in a work of a somewhat general character, the details of the statute law of the several States would be given; but, as far as practicable, the law has been noticed, so far as it affected the formalities of execution, attestation, and proof. Many of the principles of the law relating to wills are of such a general and well established character as to be adapted to every locality, and therefore it is believed this work will not have a mere local utility. As far as possible, every effort has been made to have it accurate; that there may be some minor inaccuracies is inevitable, but none, it is hoped, of a serious character.

INTRODUCTION.

The making of a last will and testament is one of the most solemn acts of a man's life. Few are so frivolous and indifferent as not to realize the importance of an act which is to live after them, and survive long after the hand that traced it has mingled with its kindred dust. They feel that, however regardless people have been of their sayings and doings, however trivial and unimportant have been their acts in the eyes of others, a certain attention, respect, and weight will be given to so deliberate and serious an act as a man's will. They realize, when making it, that they are exercising one of the highest and most important privileges society has granted to the individual—the right to speak and order as to the disposition of his effects and property after he has ceased to live. Accordingly, men who have been rudely treated by the world, whose infirmities and eccentricities have subjected them to its ridicule, whose words would command no hearing from their fellow-men, have eagerly availed themselves of this last and important opportunity to freely speak their mind, to vent their spleen on ungrateful friends, to deride an unfeeling world, and in a cynical manner to express without reserve opinions about persons and things, which could have no hearing while they lived, but in a last will and testament will command the attention due to the solemnity of the occasion. In a word, they take this method to give a parting hit to an unfriendly and unsympathizing world.

It will be instructive, as well as interesting, as a phase of human nature, to refer, by way of introduction, to some curious wills, which may form an inviting prelude to a more serious treatment of the subject.

As might be anticipated, many wills reflect the singular notions, the eccentricities and prejudices of the makers. In many cases, the testator speaks his mind so freely that his opinion of others really amounts to a libel; again, his antipathies or his affections are as freely exhibited; while the instances are not rare in which he bequeaths to posterity the benefit of his religious opinions.

Testators often give directions as to the place and manner of their burial, as well as the expenses of their funeral pageant. In one case, a testator desired to be buried in a space between the graves of his first and second wives.* Mr. Zimmerman, whose will was proved in 1840, in England, accompanied the directions for his funeral with something like a threat in case they were not carried out. In his will he says: "No person is to attend my corpse to the grave, nor is any funeral bell to be rung; and my desire is to be buried plainly and in a decent manner; *and if this be not done, I will come again*

---

* Illustrated London News, October 18th, 1873. I have selected from this reliable journal many of the examples of curious wills I give in this introduction, taken from Doctors' Commons, London.

—*that is to say, if I can.*" The Countess Dowager of Sandwich, in her will, written by herself at the age of eighty, proved in November, 1862, expresses her wish to be buried decently and quietly—*no undertakers' frauds, or cheating; no scarfs, hatbands, or nonsense.* In a similar manner, Mrs. Kitty Jenkyn Packe Reading, whose will was proved in April, 1870, gives explicit directions as to avoiding useless expense at her funeral. She died abroad, and directed that her remains be put into a leaden coffin, then enclosed in a wooden coffin, and to be taken as freight to her residence, Branksome Tower, in England. She foresaw that in this way the remains could not enter the house through the door, and directed a window to be taken out of a certain room, in order to permit her remains to enter.

The memory of the jars and ills of domestic life has so embittered a man's mind, that if the strife was unequal during his lifetime, he hopes to turn the scale in his favor when dying, and in his will have a last word, and in this way cut off his spouse from her inalienable prescriptive right of having the last word. A man, then, has been known to call his wife "jealous, disaffectionate, reproachful, and censorious." And again, a wife's faults and shortcomings have been published to the world, and children must be mortified to know that in the public documents of the country allusion is conspicuously made to the failings of their mother, as when a husband perpetuates his wife's "unprovoked, unjustifiable fits of passion, violence, and cruelty." The following words are used by an individual who died in London in June, 1791, in reference to his wife: "Seeing that I have had the misfortune to be married to the aforesaid Elizabeth, who ever since our union has tormented me in every possible way; that not content with making game of all my remonstrances, she has done all she could to render my life miserable; that Heaven seems to have sent her into the world solely to drive me out of it; that the strength of Samson, the genius of Homer, the prudence of Augustus, the skill of Pyrrhus, the patience of Job, the philosophy of Socrates, the subtlety of Hannibal, the vigilance of Hermogenes, would not suffice to subdue the perversity of her character; that no power on earth can change her, seeing we have lived apart during the last eight years, and that the only result has been the ruin of my son, whom she has corrupted and estranged from me. Weighing maturely and seriously all these circumstances, I have bequeathed, and I bequeath to my said wife, Elizabeth, the sum of *one shilling*, to be paid unto her within six months after my decease."*

Happily, the ills and strifes of conjugal life are not the most frequently remembered incidents of a man's life; its felicities, its joys and tender experiences, the fidelity and devotion of a true partner, are often most vividly and fondly cherished at death, and touchingly alluded to in a man's last will. In this manner, Sharon Turner, the eminent author of the "History of the Anglo-Saxons," and other works, who died in London in 1847, at the age of seventy-

---

* Illustrated London News, February 21st, 1874.

nine, and whose will was proved in that year, delights to speak of his wife's affection, and is particularly solicitous that she should not suffer in her personal appearance by the unskillfulness of the persons who had taken her portrait. Speaking of his wife, who was dead, he says: "It is my comfort to have remembered that I have passed with her nearly forty-nine years of unabated affection and connubial happiness, and yet she is still living, as I earnestly hope and believe, under her Saviour's care, in a superior state of being. . . . . . . None of the portraits of my beloved wife give any adequate representation of her beautiful face, nor of the sweet, and intellectual, and attractive appearance of her living features, and general countenance, and character."

Too often testators place all the obstacles they can in the way of their widows marrying again, as will appear more fully in another part of this work. The following instance is one of the few exceptions, and it contains, besides, the most graceful tribute to a wife's character, as given in a will, that we know of. Mr. Granville Harcourt, whose will was proved in March, 1862, thus speaks of his wife: "The unspeakable interest with which I constantly regard Lady Waldegrave's future fate induces me to advise her earnestly to unite herself again with some one who may deserve to enjoy the blessing of her society during the many years of her possible survival after my life. I am grateful to Providence for the great happiness I enjoy in her singular affection; and I pray and confidently hope she may long continue to possess the same esteem and friendship of those who are intimate with her, and can appreciate her admirable qualities, and the respect of all with whom, in any relation of life, she is connected."*

Ladies have not the same opportunity and privilege of restraining their husbands from marrying again, and we cannot call to mind a single case of a married woman attempting to do so in a will, but on the contrary, we have the case of a lady recommending marriage to her husband. Mrs. Van Hanrigh, whose will was proved in December, 1868, leaves all her property, which appears to have been considerable, to her husband. Endorsed on the back of the will is a memorandum, stating that she wishes her clothes to be sold to pay her funeral expenses, which are to be as small as possible, and after commending her husband to the care of her brother, she adds: "It is also my earnest wish that my darling husband should marry, ere long, a nice, pretty girl, who is a good housewife, and above all, to be careful that she is of a good temper."

Theologians have speculated and differed upon the nature of Heaven's happiness, but John Starkey, whose will was proved in November, 1861, had no doubt of its character, for he states: "The remainder of my wealth is vested in the affection of my dear wife, with whom I leave it in the good hope of resuming it more pure, bright, and precious, where neither moth nor rust doth corrupt, and where there are no railways or monetary panics or fluctuations of exchange, but the

---

* Illustrated London News. November 8th. 1873.

steadfast though progressive and unspeakable riches of glory and immortality."

The disappointments of life, the inconstancy of friends, and the slights of the world have so wrought upon some minds as to cause them to record in a will their estimate of all earthly things, and enlighten posterity by revealing to it the last impressions of either a cynic or a philosopher. Soured and chagrined, they rail at what they deem the folly and hypocrisy of the world, and in a last utterance freely express themselves upon subjects upon which, perhaps, the proprieties of life made them silent while they lived. The following document, penned by an Earl of Pembroke who lived during the political turmoils of the seventeenth century, testifies to a singular shrewdness and knowledge of character, with a considerable amount of dry humor. As a literary and historical curiosity, we may be justified in giving it at length. The copy from which it is taken bears the signature of the keeper of the records in Doctors' Commons, Nathaniel Brind, beneath the words *"Concordat cum originali."* It is as follows:

"I, Philip V, Earl of Pembroke and Montgomery, being, as I am assured, of unsound health, but of sound memory, as well I remember me that five years ago I did give my vote for the despatching of old Canterbury, neither have I forgotten that I did see my king upon the scaffold, yet as it is said that death doth even now pursue me, and, moreover, that it is yet further said that it is my practice to yield under coercion, I do now make my last will and testament.

"Imprimus: As for my soul, I do confess I have often heard men speak of the soul, but what may be these same souls, or what their destination, God knoweth; for myself, I know not. Men have likewise talked to me of another world, which I have never visited, nor do I know even an inch of the ground that leadeth thereto. When the King was reigning I did make my son wear a surplice, being desirous that he should become a bishop, and for myself, I did follow the religion of my master; then came the Scotch, who made me a Presbyterian; but since the time of Cromwell, I have become an Independent. These are, methinks, the three principal religions of the kingdom. If any one of the three can save a soul, I desire they will return it to him who gave it to me.

"Item: I give my body, for it is plain I cannot keep it, as you see the chirurgeons are tearing it to pieces. Bury me, therefore; I hold lands and churches enough for that. Above all, put not my body beneath the church porch, for I am, after all, a man of birth, and I would not that I should be interred there where Colonel Pride was born.

"Item: I will have no monument, for then I must needs have an epitaph and verses over my carcass—during my life I had enough of these.

"Item: I desire that my dogs may be shared among all the members of the Council of State. With regard to them, I have been all things to all men; sometimes went I with the Peers, sometimes with the Commons. I hope therefore they will not suffer my poor curs to want.

"Item: I give my two best saddle-horses to the Earl of Denbigh, whose legs, methinks, must soon begin to fail him. As regards my other horses, I bequeath them to Lord Fairfax, that when Cromwell and his council take away his commission, he may still have some *horse* to command.

"Item: I give all my wild beasts to the Earl of Salisbury, being very sure that he will preserve them, seeing that he refused the King a doe out of his park.

"Item: I bequeath my chaplains to the Earl of Stamford, seeing he has never had one in his employ, having never known any other than his son my Lord Gray, who, being at the same time spiritual and carnal, will engender more than one monster.

"Item: I give nothing to my Lord Saye, and I do make him this legacy willingly, because I know that he will faithfully distribute it unto the poor.

"Item: Seeing that I do menace a certain Henry Mildmay, but did not trash him, I do leave the sum of fifty pounds sterling to the lacquey that shall pay unto him my debt.

"Item: I bequeath to Thomas May, whose nose I did break at a masquerade, five shillings. My intention had been to give more; but all who have seen his history of the Parliament will consider that even this sum is too large.

"Item: I should have given to the author of the libel on women, entitled 'News of the Exchange,' threepence, to invent a yet more scurrilous mode of maligning; but, seeing that he insulteth and slandereth I know not how many honest persons, I commit the office of paying him to the same lacquey who undertaketh the arrears of Henry Mildmay. He will teach him to distinguish between honorable women and disreputable.

"Item: I give to the Lieutenant-General Cromwell one of my words, the which he must want, seeing that he hath never kept any of his own.

"Item: I give to the wealthy citizens of London, and likewise to the Presbyterians and nobility, notice to look to their skins, for, by order of the State, the garrison of Whitehall hath provided itself with poniards, and useth dark lanterns in the place of candles.

"Item: I give up the ghost."

One of the most interesting old wills, the first will registered in the English language in Doctors' Commons, is the will of Lady Alice West, proved in the year 1395.

The first will recorded there is in the year 1383, and is in Latin, as most of the very early wills are. She was the widow of Sir Thomas West. She begins thus, in the old-fashioned style: "In Dei nomine, Amen. On Thursday, that is to sey, the XV day of the moneth of Jul, in the yer of the incarnacion of our Lord Ihu Crist, a thousand and thre hundred and fourescore and fiftene—I, Alice West, lady of Hynton Martel, in hool estat of my body and in good mynde beynge, make my testament in the maner as hit folweth hereafter: In the begynnyng, I bequethe my soule to God Almighty and to his moder, Seynt Marie, and to al the seyntis of heuene, and my body to be beryed in Crischerche in the priorie of the chanones in Hamptschire by the Newe Forest wher as myne auncestres leggeth."

The wills of persons of distinction were, in spirit, much the same in the fourteenth century as at present; there are pecuniary and specific legacies to relatives, legacies to old and present servants, legacies for charitable purposes, and particular directions about the funeral and place of burial.

Dame Alice West's will is too long to give at length, but some extracts, showing the articles which at that period were so valuable as to be specifically bequeathed, the amounts of the legacies, and the persons to whom they were left, may prove interesting.

The lady commences the disposition of her property as follows: "Also, I devyse to Thomas, my sone, a bed of tapicers werk with alle the tapices of sute, red of color, ypouthered with chapes and scochons in the corners of myn auncestres armes, with that I bequethe to the same Thomas the stoffe longyng thereto—that is to seye, my best fetherbed, and a blue canevas and a materas and twey blankettys and a peyre schetes of reynes and sex of my best pilwes."

It is an unusual thing in the present day to dispose of bedding by will; and the reason is, that feather-beds, mattresses, pillows, blankets, and sheets are comparatively cheap; but in Lady Alice's time they must have been articles of luxury and a considerable item in the dower of a bride.

The testatrix next thinks of her daughter-in-law:

"Also I bequethe to Johane my sone is wyf, a masse book and alle the bokes that I have of latyn, englisch, and frensch out take the forsayd matyns book, that is bequethe to Thomas my sone."

We wonder what books she had, and particularly what English books; a list of them would be most interesting. She could not have had many, and we cannot suggest what they were. It should be remembered that this will was made more than five years before the death of Chaucer, and nearly eighty years before the first book was printed in English, and books in English must consequently have been few indeed. Their scarcity made them of great value; they were carefully treasured, and their future ownership specially provided for by will. Something might be said as to the education of ladies of the highest class at that time. Here was a lady possessing books in English, Latin, and French, which, it is presumable, she could read. Latin, however, was the language of her religion; French was probably the tongue she was brought up in, and was the language of the court; and English was the language of her dependents; so that, as a matter of course, every lady of rank may have been familiar with the three languages.

She further gives certain gifts to members of her family: "To Sir Nichol Clifton, Knyght, and to Alianore his wif, my doughter, and to Thomas Clifton here sone, £120, euenliche to be departed betwix ham thre; and if Thomas here sone forsayd deyeth, I wol that it torne to profet of his fader and his moder."

We should not expect to find any will previously to the Reformation without a legacy to say masses. Lady West gives £18 10s., "for to synge and seye 4400 masses for my lord Sir Thomas West is soule, and for myne, and for alle cristene soules," and they are to be " done " within " fourteen night after her deces." There is another bequest to Christ Church, where she was to be buried, " to bidde and to rede, and synge for my lordes soule forsayd, and myne, and alle cristene soules, while the world schal laste."

Having given all the legacies she desires, the testatrix then disposes of the remainder of her property: "An al the residue of my godes, after the dettys that I owe ben quyt, and after my testament is parfoned, I bequethe to the forsayd Thomas my sone"; and after all these directions and legacies, the good lady finishes her will by ordering the manner of her own interment; when she dies her body is to be carried to the " forsayd priorie of Crischerch, and with right litel cost" buried at the first mass, with a taper of six pounds of wax burning at her head, and another taper of six pounds of wax burning at her feet.

The will of Shakspeare, executed on the 25th March, 1616, not quite a month previous to his death, forms a most interesting document for the scholar, as well as the lawyer. It is registered in Doctors' Commons *verbatim* as it was written, and is prized as a unique and interesting document relating to the poet. It is written in the usual clerical hand of the period, on three sheets of paper, fastened at the top. Each sheet is signed by the poet, the final signature, " By me, William Shakspeare," being the most distinct. These three autographs, with two appended to deeds relating to his property in London, constitute the only undoubted signatures of Shakspeare which we at present possess.

It commences in the old way, thus:

" In the name of God, Amen! I, William Shackspeare of Stratford upon Avon, in the countie of Warr. gent, in perfect health and memorie, God be praysed! doe make and ordayne this my last will and testament in manner and forme followeing; That ys to saye, First, I comend my Soule into the handes of God my Creator, hoping and assuredlie beleeving, through thonelie merites of Jesus Christe my Saviour, to be made partaker of lyfe everlastynge, And my bodye to the Earth whereof yt ys made."

It would be tedious to give *in extenso* the various items of this celebrated will; we shall only refer to a few such items as are sufficiently remarkable. In one item he gives a bequest to his sister Joan: " I gyve and bequeath unto my said sister Jone XX pounds, and all my wearing Apparrell, to be paied and delivered within one yeare after my deceas; and I doe will and devise unto her *the house* with thappurtenaunces in Stratford wherein she dwelleth, for her natural lief, under the yearlie rent of xij^d," or twelve pence.

He gives various specific and general legacies; and, if we judge by the number of such, he must have had numerous friends. In another item he gives to the poor of Stratford "tenn poundes"; to Mr. Thomas Combe his sword; to his daughter Judith his "broad silver gilt bole." The most remarkable item in the will is the following: "*I give unto my wief my second best bed with the furniture.*" He devised to his daughter, Susanna Hall, his landed property in Stratford, limited to the first or other sons of her body after her life.

It is said the object of the poet in leaving the bulk of his property to Mrs. Hall was evidently to found a family, the darling object of Shakspeare's ambition. One clause interlined in the will has occasioned a good deal of marvel and censorious criticism—the bequest to his wife, who has been represented as cut off by him, not indeed with a shilling, but with an old bed. But, as she was entitled in law to dower out of his real estate, Shakspeare may not have deemed it necessary to make any further bequest to his wife than that of the second-best bed, as a special mark of affection. This is the explanation now tendered of what must otherwise have appeared a most extraordinary procedure on the part of the poet. It must be admitted, however, that, making full allowance for her provision by right of law, there still remains a feeling of dissatisfaction with the total exclusion of Anne Shakspeare from all parts of her husband's will, with the exception of an interlined clause of a dozen words. It is also a significant fact that, with the exception of the bed, no household furniture is bequeathed to the widow; so that she must have been left dependent on her daughters for lodging and residence.

The will of Henry VIII in some of its provisions is well worth the attention of the scholar, as it reflects the state of the distinguished testator's religious opinions, which, contrary to general impressions, were not entirely in harmony with the views of the Reformers in England. This will was the subject of judicial examination, in the House of Lords, in 1860. (8 H. L. Cas. 369.)

It appears that, by the foundation of Edward III, when he instituted the order of the Garter, and created the Poor Knights, a certain obligation had been cast upon the dean and canons of Windsor to provide for the Poor Knights, the King having promised the dean and canons lands to enable them to do so. But, by an Act of Parliament, passed in the 22 Edw. IV, reciting that "the possessions given to the said dean and canons suffice not to sustain all other charges, and also to bear the charges of the Poor Knights," it was enacted "that the same dean and canons, and their successors forever more, be utterly quit and discharged from all manner of exhibition or charge of or for any of the same Knights." Down to the end of the reign of Henry VIII, the Poor Knights appear to have been fed only with promises, and no permanent provision was made for them. In the 3 Hen. VIII, the dean and canons having, at his request, granted to a Poor Knight, named Peter Narbonne, an annuity of twenty marks for his life, the King wrote them a letter of thanks, in which he acknowledges that they were not bound to find anything for the Poor Knights since the 22 Edw. IV; thanks them for their bounty to Peter Narbonne; promises them favor in their suits hereafter as a recompense, and assures them "that they shall not be burthened with the maintenance of any other Poor Knights till such time as he should have provided lands for their exhibition, which not only should be sufficient to discharge the dean and canons of such Knights, but also of the said annuity."

The promise was not fulfilled; and when Henry's end approached; the breach of it lay heavily upon his conscience, and hence the following provision in his will, which was dated December 30th, 1546, about three weeks before his death. One of the directions was: "That, as soon as may be after our departure from this world, the Dean and Chapter shall have manors, etc., to the yearly value of £600 over all charges, made sure to them and their successors, forever, upon the conditions hereafter ensuing." Among the other provisions were the following:

"And for the due and full accomplishment and performance of all other things conteined with the same in the form of an indenture, signed with our own hand, which shall be passed by way of covenant for that purpose between the said Deane and Cannons and our executors, if it pass not between us and the said Deane and Cannons in our liefe; that is to say, the said Deane and Cannons and their successours forever shall finde two prestes to say masses at the said aulter to be made where we have before appointed our tomb to be made and stand; and also after our decease kepe yerely four solemne obites for us within the said College of Windesour, and at every of the same obites to cause a solemne sermon to be made, and also at every of the said obites to give to poor people in almes tenne poundes.

"And also to give forever yerely to thirtene poor men, who shall be called Poor Knightes, to every of them twelf pens every daye, and ones in the yere yerely forever, a long joune of white cloth, with the garter upon the brest, embrodered with a sheld and cross of Sainte George within the garter, and a mantel of red cloth, and to such one of the said thirtene Poor Knightes as shall be appointed to be hed and gouvernour of them, £3 6s. 8d. yerely forever, over and besides the said twelf pennes by the daye.

"And also to cause, every Sunday in the yere, forever, a sermon to be made forever at Windesour aforesaid, as in the said indenture and covenant shall be more fully and particularly expressed, willing, charging, and requiring our son Prince Edwarde, all our executors and counsaillors which shall be named hereafter, and all other our heirs and successours which shall be Kinges of this realme, as they will answer before Almighty God at the dredful day of judgment, that they and every of them do see that the said indenture and assurance to be made betwene us and the said Deane and Cannons, or between them and our executours, and all thinges therein conteined, may be duly put into execution, and observed and kept forever, perpetually, according to this our last will and testament."

The Archbishop of *Canterbury and the Lord Chancellor, and a great many other eminent persons, and Councillors of the Privy Council, with " our son Prince Edwarde," were appointed " executors," and, " as they must and shall answer at the day of judgment," they were required, " truly and fully to see this my last will performed in all things with as much speed and diligence as may be."

In 1547, a meeting of the executors and Privy Councillors, with the Lord Protector at their head, was assembled, and a document was drawn up which recited the material parts of the will relating to this matter, and directed that " the Barons of the Exchequer, the King's Sergeants, the Attorney and Solicitor, should deliberately peruse the whole will, and frankly declare their opinions what the executors may lawfully do, and how and in what form the said will may be lawfully executed and performed." This was done, and a special report was afterwards made, declaring that the will might be carried into effect, and stating how that might be done.

CHAPTER I.

ORIGIN AND HISTORY OF WILLS.

Jurists do not quite agree as to the full extent of a man's interest in, and control of, the property he acquires. There are different theories as to the real title to property; most all, however, agree that occupation, united with labor, is the best ground of a title to exclusive ownership of property. But how long will this ownership or control continue? During lifetime, or for a longer period? Some maintain that, by the law of nature, it only lasts during the life of the owner, and after his decease the property again becomes merged with the general stock of the public—it becomes *publici juris;* and that to permit one to order and control its disposition after he has ceased to live, is a privilege or a concession of society, and not any inherent natural right. For a large amount of property is owned in societies advanced in civilization before the right of testamentary disposition is exercised, which would show that this right is not coeval with the foundation of society or the acquisition of property, and therefore nations are not impelled to it by a natural instinct and impulse. It is claimed that the *jus disponendi* is a necessary incident of property—an inseparable quality; but if, by this term, we understand a right of disposal while a man lives, we can admit that it belongs to ownership; but it is quite a different thing when a man ceases to live; for then, naturally, he ceases to have dominion; and if he has a natural right to dispose of his goods for a short time after death, why not for millions of years?*

It is not a natural inherent right of the individual to dispose of his property after his decease; it is no more or less than a right given by positive law—a right which is founded on convenience and concession.

For a very obvious reason, we do not find this right in the early constitution of society, either given or exercised. Society, in early times, was founded on the family as the initial unit or group, which was only recognized by the State as entitled to maintenance. Naturally, by right of this principle in early society, the property acquired by an individual went into the general stock of the family, as a necessary *appanage*, and was in the name of the head of that family, and at his decease, by a principle of early law, devolved in due course upon the successor, or the *hæres* of the Roman law, who took it with all the obligations of the deceased. Society had not yet so advanced as to make the individual an object of its care and government, and recognize him as a distinct unit apart from the family; and succession—"universal succession," as it was called—to the property in the family, was the usual disposition of property. It took a long while before society permitted the individual to dispose of his property *out of his family*, because this was

* Black. II, 21.

so abnormal and unnatural as to be only dictated by caprice, passion, or prejudice, insomuch that whenever attempted among the Romans, the will was set aside as *inofficious*, and it was not permitted at all in the early English law; and even now is a presumed ground of imbecility or insanity in a testator.

The will, as we understand it, is unquestionably of Roman origin—it is purely a creature of that law, the *corpus juris*, "the public reason of the Romans." The laws of Solon only permitted wills when the testator had no children.* Among the Hindoos, the right of adoption as a succession to property effected the same purpose as a will,† while among the Teutonic nations wills were unknown, and the children inherited.‡

At first, among the Romans, a will was neither secret, revocable, nor of effect, until after death— characteristics which we necessarily associate with a will in modern times. A will then was more like a conveyance in a man's lifetime—a sale of the family rights, property, and obligations, in the presence of witnesses, to a person known as the *Emptor Familiæ*, who assumed the place of the testator as head of the family. He might be compared to an assignee under our law, with this difference, that the latter is only liable as far as he has assets. Wills were usually witnessed by seven witnesses, who sealed outside upon a thread, and after some time, deposited in the archives during the life of

---

* Thirlwall: Hist. of Greece, 187.
† Dwight's Introd. to Maine's Ancient Law.
‡ Tac. Germ. 2.

the testator, and opened in the presence of the prætor or other officer, after decease, and any person might have a copy, being matter of record.*

The Roman law did not permit the entire disposition of property by will, if a man had a family. By a law of Justinian, one-fourth, at least, was required for the children, and when there were four children, they could claim one-third, which became a general law throughout Europe.†

The Roman influence, connection, and dominion in Great Britain necessarily introduced Roman laws and usages. It was a connection lasting fully three hundred years, during which time the country was visited by Roman jurists, and the people became familiarized with the administration of the civil law, both through the civil courts and the churches. Accordingly, while wills were not in use among kindred Teutonic people in the north of Europe, they were well known and general in the Saxon period in England, where an unlimited and absolute right of devise was given. In the laws of King Canute, provision is made for the disposition of property in cases of *intestacy*, which makes it evident that testamentary dispositions were recognized; ‡ and Canute himself left a will. § There are notices of some twenty-five Anglo-Saxon wills extant. Nearly all of the testators were people of prominence and distinction, and these wills are preserved in monastic houses to which they devised property. King Alfred's will, from its antiquity

---

* Dig. lib. 28, tit. 2.   ‡ Selden : Orig. Prob. Juris., 15.
† Spence: Eq. Juris. I, 188.   § Milton, p. 318.

and its formal character, is one of the most interesting ancient documents existing. (He died A. D. 900.) It opens thus: "I, Alfred, King by God's grace, and with Ethered's the Archbishop's counsel, and all the West Saxon Wights, witness, have considered about my soul's thrift, and about the inheritance that to me, God and mine Ancestors did give, and about the inheritance that Ethulf, King, my father to us, three brothers, bequeathed, Ethelbold, Etherad and me." He provides for masses thus: "And so divide for me and my father, and for the friends that be interceded for, and I intercede for, two hundred of pounds, fifty to the mass priests over all my kingdom, fifty to God's poor ministers, fifty to the distressed poor, fifty to the church that I at shall rest; and know not certainly whether the money so much is, nor I know not but of it more may be, but so I ween."

It appears that King Alfred's will was prepared by the Archbishop's counsel, and published in the presence of the West Saxon Wights, or Wise Men. This gives us a glimpse at the interference of the clergy in such important affairs, and leads us on a most interesting and important inquiry as to the connection of wills with ecclesiastical courts.

The clergy of that time possessed a monopoly of the learning of the day, and especially of the learning of the civil law, having made it a matter of study. Reasonably they would be consulted on subjects on which the civil or Roman law had such a bearing; and as a matter of fact, they soon became presiding judges with the civil magistrate in cases of probate of wills. In the early Saxon period, the bishop sat with the earl in the county court in the administration of testamentary matters; and this was the case up to the time of the Normans. But the clergy had occasion to interfere on other grounds, at a very early period. At a very early day, they sought jurisdiction in probate matters. The practice was probably favored by the sanction given by the civil law to the intervention of the bishop to compel the execution of a will where there were legacies *in pios usus*—to pious uses.* When any legacy was disposed of to pious uses, for the use of the church, for monasteries, or for the poor, the bishops were to sue for the same, and see to the administration thereof.† But Justinian would not allow further than this, and he prohibited the bishops interfering generally in the probate of wills.‡ Upon which a writer remarks: "Here we see the clergy in those days had set their foot upon the business, and I suppose since that time they never pulled it wholly out again."

The popes, as their power increased, endeavored to obtain the jurisdiction over testaments. Pope Innocent the Fourth claimed for the bishop the power to dispense property left to a charity, if there be no executor appointed by the will, and if there be an executor, and he does not discharge the duty faithfully, the bishop may assume administration.§

As a matter of history, in European countries,

---

* Selden, pp. 3, 4.   ‡ Idem, leg. 41.
† Code: lib. I, tit. 3, leg. 42.   § Decret. lib. 3, tit. 26, C. 19.

except England, the church did not pretend that wills were of ecclesiastical cognizance *sua natura*, but only such wills as were made for pious uses.* So that the origin of the jurisdiction of ecclesiastical courts touching testamentary matters is by the custom of England, and not by ecclesiastical law. Blackstone says: "The spiritual jurisdiction of testamentary causes is a peculiar constitution of this island; for in almost all other (even in popish) countries all matters testamentary are under the jurisdiction of the civil magistrate." †

We have seen that during the Saxon period the bishop presided with the earl in the administration of testamentary matters; but in the eighteenth year of William the Conqueror, a separate court was organized for the bishop, who no longer sat with the civil authorities. This was the beginning of the ecclesiastical jurisdiction; though at first power was granted only to adjudicate on such matters as were for the good of the soul, an expression which the bishops subsequently made very elastic and comprehensive. The clergy did not acquire the exclusive jurisdiction till the reign of Henry I, who by charter first established this jurisdiction.‡ In the time of Richard I, when he was in confinement, the clergy were more fully established in this right, for they obtained from him a confirmation of the ecclesiastical immunities. §

The proof of wills was thus well settled and established, for it is spoken of as an ordinary and un-

---

* Marriot v. Marriot, 1 Strange 667.
† Black. III, 95.
‡ Matt. Paris, fo. 56.
§ Idem, fo. 161.

disputed usage, and through all the animated disputes in the reign of Henry II, as to the civil and ecclesiastical jurisdiction, it is observable that nothing is advanced against the authority of the spiritual courts in testamentary causes. In the reign of Richard II the county courts were prohibited to infere with the probate of wills.*

By the early common law of England, if a man had a wife and children, he had only a testamentary disposition of one-third of his property; the remainder, the shares of the widow and children, were called *rationabiles partes*, which must be intact. The personal attendance of the clergy on the dying would ordinarily lead to the disposition of the third which a person was privileged to bequeath by testament; and, from ancient wills, it is very evident this power was liberally and generally exercised in favor of religious uses, such as were deemed for the soul's health of the testator. Whenever, by accident or extreme feebleness, the exercise of this right was prevented, the third thus left at the disposal of a person was of right claimed by the clergy, as the "dead man's part," to be appropriated for his benefit, *pro animæ salute*. This would lead to the intervention of the spiritual courts in the distribution of an intestate's estate, especially as they had full power over the probate. So it became the invariable custom to take the third of an intestate's goods for pious uses, which were, to assist in paying for masses for the benefit of the

* 1 Strange 667.

"defunct's soul," to assist the poor and infirm, to pay for church lights, religious services, and anniversaries. If a man died without wife or children, the Ordinary, as the bishop was termed, had the administration of the whole of an intestate's property, subject to the payment of the debts of the deceased. It is easy to see what immense power and revenue accrued to the church in consequence of the establishment of these privileges; and the influence gained thereby, and the flagrant abuses resulting from this prerogative, caused just alarm to the civil power, and led to a struggle to curtail such powers in the reign of Edward III,* when a law was passed providing that the Ordinary should grant the administration to the next of kin. The Statute of Distribution, in the reign of Charles II, destroyed the old common-law right to the *pars rationabilis*, and made the estate distributable among the widow and next of kin, leaving still, however, in the hands of the administrator, for his own use, the third formerly retained by the church; and finally, by statute, in the first year of James II, it was provided that this third should also be distributed. So, after a struggle of many years, the administration of the goods of an intestate was taken out of the hands of the spiritual courts, and rightfully given to the family of the deceased. The long, slow process is an interesting phase of history for the general reader, as it is for the lawyer, who finds it necessary to follow it, because the rules and

---

*Black. II, ch. 32.

decisions of the ecclesiastical courts as to the probate of wills and the administration of personal property have become incorporated into the body of our law, and form a part of it.*

Up to the thirty-second year of Henry VIII, there was no power to make a will of real estate. In his reign the Statute of Wills was passed, which first gave this power, and after that time a person had the right to make wills of real as well as personal property; but the ecclesiastical courts had only cognizance of the wills of personal property; the common-law courts had the jurisdiction of wills relating to real estate.

The next statute that affected wills was the *Statute of Frauds*, in the twenty-ninth year of Charles II, which required wills affecting real estate to be in writing, *signed* by the testator, and attested in the presence of three or four credible witnesses. This statute had an immense influence on our jurisprudence, and is substantially adopted in all our States, with slight variations.† In that statute certain formalities were insisted upon, but only in regard to a will of real estate; a will of personal property was not required to be executed in the same manner and with the like formalities. ‡ Before the Statute of Frauds, according to 32 Henry VIII, it was only necessary for the will to be in

---

* Hale, Hist. of Com. Law, 28.
† Greenleaf, Evid., vol. I, § 26.
‡ Lord Hardwicke, in Ross v. Ewer, 3 Atk. 156, said: "There is nothing that requires so little solemnity as the making of a will of personal estate. There is scarcely any paper writing that will not be admitted as such.

writing; and accordingly, where a man beyond the sea wrote a letter, in which he declared his will to be that his land should go in a certain way, it was adjudged a good will.* And a will written without the appointment of the testator, if read to him and approved by him, was held good, signing and sealing not being necessary.†

Now, by statute I Vict., ch. 26, in England, there are required the same formalities in a will of personal estate as by the Statute of Frauds are required in a will of real estate, and the same is now the case in nearly all our States; and, by the same statute, a person has a full testamentary disposition of all real estate, as well as personal, to which he is entitled, either in law or in equity, at the time of his death.

Our American States generally, after the Revolution, adopted the English common law, as it was at certain periods—some taking one date, and others a different one; but in all substantially the common law was taken as the foundation of our municipal law, with the exception of Louisiana. Hence the law relating to the execution and probate of wills, as administered in the ecclesiastical courts, was engrafted here, subject to certain statutory modifications suitable to our polity and circumstances. But we, having no recognition of an established religion, have given this jurisdiction to special civil courts, denominated Probate Courts in some States, as in California; the Orphan's Court, as in New

* Moore, 177. † Cro. Eliz. 100.

Jersey; the Surrogate's Court, as in New York. The name Surrogate again brings to our mind a reminiscence of the former ecclesiastical jurisdiction; it was the name given to the bishop's deputy. However, in all, no matter by what name known, the precedents, the decisions, and rules, as established in the ecclesiastical courts in England, in regard to testamentary matters, have authority and force; and it is for this reason the history and adjudication of these courts are so necessary to the lawyer of the present day.*

* It should be observed that the ecclesiastical jurisdiction over wills is now abolished in England; and, since 1857, the jurisdiction is given to the Court of Probate and Divorce.

very sick, weak, and past all hope of recovery." Chancellor Kent says: "This has been the uniform language of the English law-writers from that time to this day, so that it has become the acknowledged doctrine, that a nuncupative will is only to be tolerated when made *in extremis*."*

The danger of collusion and conspiracy among those who surround a feeble dying person has taught legislatures to be very strict in placing adequate safeguards around such a one. It was a gross abuse of such an opportunity, in a remarkable case in the twenty-eighth year of Charles II, that led, it is supposed, to the enactment of the Statute of Frauds in the next year.

The case was this:† Mr. Cole, at a very advanced age, married a young woman, who during her lifetime did not conduct herself so as to make the old man's life a placid or a happy one. After his death she set up a nuncupative will, said to have been made *in extremis*, by which the whole estate was given to her, in opposition to a will made three years before the testator's death, giving £3,000 to charitable uses. The nuncupative will was proved by nine witnesses; and after examination in the course of a trial, it appeared most of the witnesses were perjured, and Mrs. Cole was found guilty of subornation. It was then that Lord Nottingham said: "I hope to see one day a law that no written will should be revoked but by writing." He was gratified in seeing such a law the succeeding year.

* 20 Johns. 511.   † Cole v. Mordaunt, 4 Ves. 196.

Upon this, Chancellor Kent observed: " I should hope to see one day a law that no nuncupative will should be valid in any case." *

The case in which these words were used was a very curious one, and will be worth while to be stated somewhat fully. We can give no better statement of it than the admirable summary given by that eminent jurist in his opinion, where the subject of nuncupative wills received a thorough discussion. The will was made by a William Jones on the 11th April, 1820, and was as follows: " I now say, as I have repeatedly said before, that I leave all the property I am possessed of to Mary Hazleton; I do this in consequence of the good treatment and kind attention I have received from her during my sickness. She is worthy of it. No other person shall inherit my property. I wish you all in the room to take notice of this." The will was witnessed by four witnesses. It was finally declared invalid, because it did not appear the testator made it in his last extremity, and as there were so many evidences of undue influence. The facts were as given by Kent: " William Jones was an Irishman by birth and a religious Catholic by profession. He was born in the county of Dublin, in Ireland, and received a school education about thirty years before his death, and which carries us back to the year 1790. He had then living parents, brothers, and sisters, and he was the youngest of the family. He was apprenticed to a house carpen-

* Prince v. Hazleton, 20 Johns. 513.

CHAPTER II.

Form and Requisites of Wills.

A will, from its nature, is the declaration of a man's mind as to the proper disposition of his property after death. This declaration, as any other fact, is established by evidence, oral or written. It is not the essence of a will that it shall be in writing; the essence is the declared purpose or intention, and this is established, as any other fact in law, by witnesses, or by the written declaration of the testator. In Bacon's Abridgement, a will, therefore, is defined to be, "A declaration of the mind, either by word or writing, in disposing of an estate; and to take place after the death of the testator."* A distinction was formerly made between a will and a testament; when lands or tenements were devised in writing, it was by will, and when goods and chattels were disposed of, it was by testament; but this distinction is now lost sight of, and the words are used indiscriminately, and we speak of the posthumous disposition of an estate, of whatever kind, as by last will and testament.

Since peculiar perils and obstacles beset a man in his last hours; as much uncertainty and contention have arisen as to his precise purpose and declaration; and as there is a strong and very unusual

---

* Wills—A.

temptation and opportunity given to designing and evil persons who may surround him, to falsify his intention to their advantage, it has seemed politic and wise to legislatures to prescribe a mode by which wills shall be evidenced and proved, to guard against fraud, imposition, and uncertainty. Hence, in the statutory enactments of every State, there are precise and strict rules laid down on the subject; and as writing is the most reliable and permanent mode of conveying the proof of a person's intention; and as it is now an acquirement possessed by almost every one, it is now the mode insisted on for embodying the declaration of a man's last will and testament, with rare exceptions as to verbal wills. We may, therefore, speak of wills in two great classes, viz., *Verbal* and *Written.*

Section 1.—Nuncupative Wills.

A nuncupative will is a verbal declaration of a person's intention as to the manner of disposition of his property after death. Formerly, at an early period, this must have been the usual kind of will in general use, when writing was a rare acquirement. Before the Statute of Frauds, it was of as great force and efficacy (except for lands, tenements, and hereditaments) as a written testament.* But as wills of this kind were found liable to great impositions and frauds, and occasioned many perjuries, that statute placed them under several restrictions,

---

* Swinb. Pt. I, Sec. 12.

except when made by "any soldier in actual military service, or any mariner or seaman being at sea."*

The imminent dangers, the diseases and sudden death which constantly beset soldiers and sailors; the utter inability oftentimes to find the time or the means to make a deliberate or written testamentary disposition of their effects, seem at all times to have made them a proper exception to the operation of a rule which the wisdom of later times has found it expedient, if not absolutely obligatory, to apply to all others. Hence, almost all governments grant this immunity to this class of persons. It was a peculiar privilege of the Roman soldiers, who were exempt when on a military expedition from complying with the strict testamentary law; the privilege, however, was only well established under the Empire, and after a time it was extended to the naval service, and officers, rowers, and sailors were, in this respect, esteemed as soldiers.†

Another class of persons formerly permitted to make this kind of will were those who were at the point of death, or as it was termed, *in extremis*. And in many States this privilege is still granted this class.

For a long period, as far back as a little before the time of Henry VIII, this kind of will was confined to this class of persons.‡ A writer of the time of Henry VIII says: "This kind of testament is made commonly when the testator is now

---

* 29 Car. II, Ch. 3, Sec. 23. † Dig. lib. 37, tit. 12, Sec. 1.
‡ Redfield on Wills, I, p. 184.

very sick, weak, and past all hope of recovery." Chancellor Kent says: "This has been the uniform language of the English law-writers from that time to this day, so that it has become the acknowledged doctrine, that a nuncupative will is only to be tolerated when made *in extremis.*"[*]

The danger of collusion and conspiracy among those who surround a feeble dying person has taught legislatures to be very strict in placing adequate safeguards around such a one. It was a gross abuse of such an opportunity, in a remarkable case in the twenty-eighth year of Charles II, that led, it is supposed, to the enactment of the Statute of Frauds in the next year.

The case was this:[†] Mr. Cole, at a very advanced age, married a young woman, who during her lifetime did not conduct herself so as to make the old man's life a placid or a happy one. After his death she set up a nuncupative will, said to have been made *in extremis,* by which the whole estate was given to her, in opposition to a will made three years before the testator's death, giving £3,000 to charitable uses. The nuncupative will was proved by nine witnesses; and after examination in the course of a trial, it appeared most of the witnesses were perjured, and Mrs. Cole was found guilty of subornation. It was then that Lord Nottingham said: "I hope to see one day a law that no written will should be revoked but by writing." He was gratified in seeing such a law the succeeding year.

[*] 20 Johns. 511. [†] Cole v. Mordaunt, 4 Ves. 196.

CURIOSITIES OF WILLS.

Jersey; the Surrogate's Court, as in New York. The name Surrogate again brings to our mind a reminiscence of the former ecclesiastical jurisdiction; it was the name given to the bishop's deputy. However, in all, no matter by what name known, the precedents, the decisions, and rules, as established in the ecclesiastical courts in England, in regard to testamentary matters, have authority and force; and it is for this reason the history and adjudication of these courts are so necessary to the lawyer of the present day.*

* It should be observed that the ecclesiastical jurisdiction over wills is now abolished in England; and, since 1857, the jurisdiction is given to the Court of Probate and Divorce.

CHAPTER II.

Form and Requisites of Wills.

A will, from its nature, is the declaration of a man's mind as to the proper disposition of his property after death. This declaration, as any other fact, is established by evidence, oral or written. It is not the essence of a will that it shall be in writing; the essence is the declared purpose or intention, and this is established, as any other fact in law, by witnesses, or by the written declaration of the testator. In Bacon's Abridgement, a will, therefore, is defined to be, "A declaration of the mind, either by word or writing, in disposing of an estate; and to take place after the death of the testator."* A distinction was formerly made between a will and a testament; when lands or tenements were devised in writing, it was by will, and when goods and chattels were disposed of, it was by testament; but this distinction is now lost sight of, and the words are used indiscriminately, and we speak of the posthumous disposition of an estate, of whatever kind, as by last will and testament.

Since peculiar perils and obstacles beset a man in his last hours; as much uncertainty and contention have arisen as to his precise purpose and declaration; and as there is a strong and very unusual

Upon this, Chancellor Kent observed: "I should hope to see one day a law that no nuncupative will should be valid in any case."*

The case in which these words were used was a very curious one, and will be worth while to be stated somewhat fully. We can give no better statement of it than the admirable summary given by that eminent jurist in his opinion, where the subject of nuncupative wills received a thorough discussion. The will was made by a William Jones on the 11th April, 1820, and was as follows: "I now say, as I have repeatedly said before, that I leave all the property I am possessed of to Mary Hazleton; I do this in consequence of the good treatment and kind attention I have received from her during my sickness. She is worthy of it. No other person shall inherit my property. I wish you all in the room to take notice of this." The will was witnessed by four witnesses. It was finally declared invalid, because it did not appear the testator made it in his last extremity, and as there were so many evidences of undue influence. The facts were as given by Kent: "William Jones was an Irishman by birth and a religious Catholic by profession. He was born in the county of Dublin, in Ireland, and received a school education about thirty years before his death, and which carries us back to the year 1790. He had then living parents, brothers, and sisters, and he was the youngest of the family. He was apprenticed to a house carpen-

---

* Prince v. Hazleton, 20 Johns. 513.

ter in the city of Dublin, and served a regular apprenticeship of seven years. When this service expired, he worked as a journeyman for nine or twelve months, and then emigrated to the United States. This brings us in the history of his life to the year 1798, and perhaps that fact may enable us to give some probable solution of the only circumstance that seems (if we except the will) to cast any shade over the memory of this man. I allude to the change of his paternal name, *O'Connor*, for that of *Jones*. It does not appear precisely when he changed his name, but I refer it back to that period as the probable time, and presume that he and his family were more or less implicated in the rebellion in Ireland in 1798, in consequence of an ill-fated attempt to effect a revolution in that kingdom. It is probable that he may have emigrated for safety; and, for greater safety, laid down the name of *O'Connor*, which was then memorable in the Irish annals, on the side of the unfortunate. But be this conjecture as it may, we find him first at New York, then for two years at Savannah, then living for twelve or fourteen years in Cuba, and learning the Spanish language, and where he probably made his fortune. He is next traced on his return to the United States to the cities of Baltimore, Philadelphia, and New York; and in all of them he seems to have had business, pecuniary concerns, and friends. These are the few and imperfect sketches of his biography to be selected from the case, before we find him rich in the fruits of his enterprise, but sick with a disease of the liver, at the boarding-house of Mrs. Fox, in Cherry street, in New York, the latter end of March, 1820.

"Jones, while at the house of Mrs. Fox, claimed to be worth altogether $65,000 in property existing in New York, Philadelphia, Baltimore, and the Island of Cuba; and to show that this claim had pretty fair pretensions to truth, there were actually found at his lodgings, at his death, bank-books showing deposits to his credit in one or more banks of New York to between thirteen and fourteen thousand dollars.

"He had been sick at Mrs. Fox's about five weeks when he is said to have made the will now under consideration. During that time he had one Ellen Taylor, a colored woman, for his hired nurse; and there was a Mrs. Hazleton, who had rooms and boarded in the same house, who also acted as his nurse. Whether Jones ever saw or heard of Mrs. H. before he came to board there, does not appear, nor have we in the case any distinct lineaments of the character which Mrs. H. sustains, or the business or purpose of her life. She was able, all at once, and without any remarkable display of goodness or any adequate cause, to gain a wonderful ascendancy over the affections of this sick man. If her story be true, and the will genuine, she obliterated from Jones' breast the sense of friendship, the charities of religion, the deep-rooted traces of national affection, every tender recollection of the ties of blood, of his natal soil, of the school-fellows of his youth, of father and mother, brother and sister, relative and friend. He was persuaded at one nod to pour the accumulated treasures of his varied life into the lap of this mysterious woman— the acquaintance of a day!"

From the manifest evils arising from this kind of wills, legislatures are not disposed to favor them; they seem only adapted to a ruder condition of society than the one we now live in. So, in the Statute of Wills in England, passed in 1838,* such wills are declared invalid, except as to soldiers and sailors; and the same is the case in nearly all our American States. But a few States still permit such wills made by persons *in extremis,* and bequeathing a limited amount of property. They are not permitted in New York, except, as in the English statute, to soldiers and sailors on actual service.† They are in California of property to one thousand dollars, and then must be proved by two witnesses, one of whom is requested by the decedent to be a witness; and the will must be reduced to writing within thirty days after death, and proved within six months after the same was uttered. ‡

Even as to soldiers and sailors great strictness is required. In the first place, soldiers must be on actual military service. The military testament was first conceded by Julius Cæsar to all soldiers, but it was subsequently limited by Justinian to those engaged on an expedition; § and our courts in modern times have invariably adhered to the principle that there must be actual warfare.

* 1 Vict. ch. 26. ‡ Civil Code, 1289-90
† 2 R. S. 60. § Code, lib. 6, tit. 21.

In this country, the cases upon the subject of nuncupative wills are considerably numerous since the last civil war. In a late case, where the deceased, a soldier, had been duly mustered into the United States service during the late civil war, and while in camp wrote a letter to a friend, directing the disposition of the amount due upon certain securities left in his hands among the brothers and sisters of the deceased, as the holder should think proper, and that all his other property should go to his wife, naming her, she paying his debts, and soon after started on an expedition or raid against Richmond, in which he was made prisoner, and soon after died in prison, the will was held good as a nuncupative one, and entitled to probate.*

Sailors must be actually serving on shipboard. Thus, in the case of Lord Hugh Seymour, the commander-in-chief of the naval force at Jamaica, but who had his official residence on shore, it was held that he did not properly come within the exception, for that he was not "at sea" within the meaning of that expression, and that a nuncupative will made by him was not valid.† It was held in New York that a person employed as cook on board of a steamship should be classed as a mariner at sea, and therefore entitled to make a nuncupative will. ‡

* Leathers v. Greenacre, 53 Maine 561.
† 2 Curteis 339.
‡ 4 Bradf. 154.

Section 2.—Written Wills.

The statute law of almost every civilized state at the present time requires a will of real and personal property to be in writing, with the exceptions noticed in the first section of this chapter. A will, wholly written by the testator, signed and dated by him, is called a *holographic will*, and is, in some States, valid, without the usual formalities required to prove wills.*

The law has not made requisite to the validity of a will that it should assume any particular form, or be couched in language technically appropriate to its testamentary character. It is sufficient that the instrument, however irregular in form, or inartifi-

---

* Such a will is valid in California, Louisiana, Tennessee, and North Carolina. In the case of Clarke v. Ransome, decided in the Supreme Court, California, October, 1875, the following document was on this ground held to be testamentary in its character:

"Dear Old Nance :—I wish to give you my watch, two shawls, and also $5,000.   Your old friend,   E. A. Gordon."

It appeared in evidence that for some years Mrs. Gordon and Miss Ransome, who was the person meant by "dear old Nance," had been on terms of intimacy. Mrs. Gordon had previously executed a will, by which she had devised to her brother the whole of the estate, with the exception of several specific legacies, one of which was to Miss Ransome for $1,000. It further appeared that after the will had been duly made and executed, Mrs. Gordon desired to make a further provision for Miss Ransome, and for that purpose drew up, wholly in her own handwriting, and delivered to Miss Ransome, the paper above propounded as a will. The court held that this paper should be admitted to probate as a testamentary instrument; but against this Chief Justice Wallace gave a dissenting opinion, on the ground that the paper was the mere expression of a wish, and was not intended by the decedent to operate as a will.

Vide Pacific Law Rep., Nov. 9, 1875.

cial in expression, discloses the intention of the maker respecting the posthumous destination of his property; and if this appears to be the nature of its contents, the instrument is regarded as a will, if otherwise witnessed according to the mode pointed out in the statute. Professional practice, and long-continued custom, however, have established some technical forms of expression. As if to appropriately mark the solemnity of the act, and to declare a consciousness of it, it was the usual way to commence a will, and it is still observed, with—" In the name of God, Amen"; but this expression is now considered too formal and quaint, and of late the practice is to introduce a will in a less formal manner, thus: " I, John Doe, of ———, in the State of ———, do hereby make and publish this my last will and testament, hereby revoking all former wills by me at any time made."

It was also customary to refer to the bodily and mental condition of the testator, as, " I, A B, being of infirm health, but of sound mind and disposing memory, and aware of the uncertainty of life, do now make, etc."; but this, to a great extent, is abrogated.

Usually, the first direction given is as to the payment of debts and funeral expenses; but this is merely formal and unnecessary, as the law would have this done in any event; but it may be of use to show that the subject of the testator's debts was brought distinctly to his mind, and may thus aid in the construction of the will.* A very general clause

---

* Redfield on Wills, I, p. 675.

in a will, without many exceptions, is one appointing one or more executors. Formerly, it was considered indispensable to the validity of a will that an executor should be named in it;* but that opinion no longer obtains either here or in England;† and now where the appointment of an executor is omitted in a will, administration is granted to a person with the will annexed.

Many may have an idea that a formal will requires a seal, no doubt from the ordinary phraseology at the close of a will, "Signed, sealed, and published," but there is no State we know of where a seal is now necessary except in New Hampshire.‡ The use of a seal, however, will be required when a testator exercises a power of appointment in a will derived from any prior will or settlement;§ but if the seal be omitted it will not render the will void; it will only render the execution void as far as the power is concerned. For instance: if, by an instrument under seal, a power is given to a married woman in the nature of an appointment to devise certain real estate, in such a case she will be required to execute the will with a seal, if the appointment is to be a valid one.

The ecclesiastical courts in England and the courts here do not confine the testamentary disposition to a single instrument, but they will consider papers of different nature and forms, if not incon-

---

* Swimb. Pt. I, Sec. 3.
† Redfield on Wills, I, p. 5.
‡ N. H. Rev. Stat. Ch. 156, Sec. 6.
§ Hight v. Wilson, 1 Dall. 94; Arndt v. Arndt, 1 S. & R. 256.

sistent, as constituting altogether the will of the deceased.* It is immaterial in what language a will is written, whether in English, or in Latin, French, or any other tongue.†

While a will is to be in writing,‡ the law insists upon certain solemnities in its execution to properly evidence the testator's act and intention, without which the will is absolutely void; and courts very strictly construe these requirements, because they are remedial, in order to guard against very grave perils and mischief. The Statute of Frauds required that all devises and bequests of any lands or tenements should be in writing, signed by the testator, or by some other person in his presence, and by his express direction, and subscribed in his presence by three or four credible witnesses. This statute has been the model on which all our statutes, relating to the proof of wills in the different States, were

* Campbell v. Logan, 2 Bradf. 90.
† Swimb., Pt. 4, Sec. 25.
‡ The statute of Pennsylvania requires every will to "be in writing," and the curious question was recently presented to the Court of Common Pleas of Chester County, whether a writing on a slate, intended by the decedent to be her last will and testament, came within the statute. The court thought the case not within the spirit of the statute, because a slate was neither intended for nor adapted to writing of a permanent character. The rule has been carried quite far enough by the admission to probate of wills written with lead pencils, as was done in Dyer's Estate, 3 Ecc. E. 92, and in Dickson v. Dickson, 1 Id. 229. In 21 P F. Smith, 454, it was thought that a will should not be written or signed in pencil, on account of the facility of alteration; but the point was not decided. In Merritt v. Clason, 12 Johns. 102, a memorandum required by the Statute of Frauds, written with a lead pencil, was held sufficient, and in Clason v. Bailey, 14 Johns. 484, this point was affirmed. In Rymes v. Clarkson, 1 Phillim. 22, it was ruled that a codicil written in pencil was valid. See also Geary v. Physic, 5 Barn. and Cress. 234, and McDowell v. Chambers, 1 Strobh. Eq. 347.

framed. Some have copied it literally, others have adopted it with certain necessary modifications. Questions had arisen under this statute as to what the legislature meant by the word "signed"; namely, whether it should be construed in its strict sense, and by analogy to other instruments, or whether it should be liberally expounded and left open as a question of construction upon intention to be inferred from the facts and circumstances attending each particular case. The construction had been, as well in the courts of England as here, that the writing of the name of the testator in the body of the will, if written by himself, with the intent of giving validity to the will, was a sufficient *signing* within the statute.* Thus the old law stood, and the mischief of it was, that it was not necessary for the testator to have adopted the instrument after it was finished, by actually signing the same at the close of the will, and it did not denote clearly that he had perfected and completed it. To remedy this evil, and to prevent future controversy as to whether a will signed by the testator in any other part of the instrument than at the *end*, denoted a complete and perfect instrument, statutes have been passed in some States requiring the will to be *subscribed* by the testator at the end thereof. The statute passed in England in the first year of Victoria, requires that the will "shall be signed at the foot or end thereof by the testator, or by some other person, in his presence and by his direction."

---

* Jarman on Wills, 70.

Notwithstanding the language of the Statute of Frauds as to *signing*, without indicating how or where, is still retained in the statutes of the majority of our States, except in Arkansas, California, Connecticut, Kentucky, and New York, where it is to be *subscribed* at the end, and in Ohio, Pennsylvania, and West Virginia, where it is to be *signed at the end* of the will.

The requirements of the New York statute are as strict, if not the strictest, of any of our States; and those of California are substantially the same by the recent civil code of that State.*

The statute is in its terms perfectly explicit. Four distinct ingredients must enter into and together constitute one entire complete act, essential to the complete execution of the instrument as a will. 1. There must be a signing by the testator at the end of the will; 2. The signing must take place in the presence of each of the witnesses, or be acknowledged to have been made in their presence; 3. The testator at the time of signing and acknowledging the writing shall declare it to be his last will; and 4. There must be two witnesses who shall sign at the end, at the request of the testator.†

There must be a concurrence of all these four requisites to give validity to the act, and the omission of either is fatal. Neither of the four, which united make a valid execution of a will, may be done at a different time from the rest. If the in-

---

* Civil Code, 1276. † 2 Rev. Stat. 63.

strument has in fact been signed at a previous time, then the signature must be acknowledged to the subscribing witnesses, which is deemed to be equivalent to a new signing of the instrument.* They cannot all be done at the same instant of time, for that is impracticable; but at the same interview, one act immediately following the other, without any interval, and without any interruption to the continuous chain of the transaction.†

We shall now refer to cases bearing on each of these requisites; and it will be seen that while the courts have with commendable firmness insisted upon a rigid compliance with the formula prescribed by the statute, they have never held that a literal compliance was necessary. No particular form of words is required to comply with the statute. The only sure guide is to look at the substance, sense, and object of the law, and with the aid of these lights endeavor to ascertain whether there has been a substantial compliance.

It is sometimes still a matter of controversy as to what may be considered a subscription or signing of the will at the end or foot thereof. In Tonnele v. Hall,‡ the writing of the instrument propounded for probate commenced on the first of several sheets of paper stitched together immediately below a margin, in this form: "In the name of God, Amen. I, John Tonnele, of the City of New York being of sound mind and memory, and

---

* Doe v. Roe, 2 Barb. 200.
† Seguine v. Seguine, 2 Barb. 385, 395.
‡ 4 Comst. 140.

considering the uncertainty of life, do make, publish, and declare this to be my last will and testament, in manner and form following, that is to say,"—and was continued on that and the four succeeding sheets. At the end of one of the sheets was the signature, and following was the usual attestation clause, signed by three witnesses. The next sheet was entirely blank, and was succeeded by a sheet on which was written, "Map of the property of John Tonnele in the Ninth and Sixteenth Wards, etc." And also written on the same, " Reduced map on file in the Register's office in the City of New York." The map indicated the position, by numbers, etc., of various lots of land in the City of New York which the will purposed to dispose of, but it was not signed by the testator nor by the witnesses. In several clauses of the will devising the real estate, reference was made to the aforesaid map; but not to the *copy* of the map annexed. The point taken in opposition to the will was, that the execution of the instrument was not in conformity to the first and fourth requisites of the statute; because, as was insisted, it was neither *subscribed* by John Tonnele, nor signed by the witnesses at the *end* of it. It was contended, that as the map annexed should be regarded as a component part of the instrument, at the time of its execution, and as it was written on the last sheet of the papers composing the instrument, it was necessarily the end of the instrument, where the subscription by the testator and the signing of the witnesses should have been made. It was held by the Court of Appeals that the will was subscribed by the testator *at the end of the will*, within the meaning and intent of the statute, and that the execution thereof was valid.

In the case of the will of Catharine Kerr before the Surrogate of New York,* the closing portion of the will and the signature were as follows:

"To the children of Mary Dow, residing in Ireland in County Kilkenny, Give and bequeath two hundred dollars to be equally divided between them. If there be a balance, my executors will divide it among my relations that are not herein mentioned. CATHE^{RIN} KEER.

"I hereby appoint Mich'l ^{Phelan} of 2nd st., and John Kelly of 9th. st., as my executors to this my last will and testament.

Witnesses, R. KEIN,
  MATTHEW M. SMITH."

"I hereby order my executors to pay all my lawful and debts & funeral expenses—should it please the Almighty now to call me. This they will do before paying any legacy above mentioned.

CATH^E KEER."

There was a question as to the genuineness of the subscription, the two witnesses calling her Keer, and the two subscriptions being of that name, her Christian name, Catherine, being abbreviated, whilst her real name was Kerr; and several previous papers were produced, in which her name, proved to have been signed by herself, was invariably written Cath-

---

* McGuire v. Kerr, 2 Bradf. 244.

erine Kerr, in full. The Surrogate held that the form of the will was fatally defective, because the will was not subscribed by the testatrix and signed by the attesting witnesses at the end, in conformity with the requirements of the statute.

The next requisite is that the testator shall sign the will in the presence of the witnesses, or acknowledge his signature to them, if it has been signed previously. The New York statute does not require the witnesses to sign in the presence of the testator, as the California statute does.* Hence, a difference of opinion has arisen as to whether the New York statute is satisfied if a testator signs a will at one time, and afterwards acknowledges it to the witnesses separately at different times. There is an opinion that the witnesses must be present at the same time, and when the testator subscribes or acknowledges the instrument;† but it has been laid down, in the case of Butler v. Benson,‡ that a separate acknowledgment is sufficient. However that may be, no careful practitioner will ever have a will executed except when both the witnesses are present; and the attestation clause generally expresses that the witnesses signed in the presence of each other.

In Whitbeck v. Patterson,§ William Patterson, the testator, signed the will in the presence of one Hughes, who had prepared it for him, but who did

---

* Civil Code, 1276.
† Dayton on Surrog. p. 76.
‡ 1 Barb. 533. It is claimed he may subscribe in presence of one, and acknowledge it separately to the other. 4 Kent, 516; 36 N. Y. 416.
§ 10 Barb. 608.

not sign it as a witness. The two then went to a store, where they found the three persons who signed as witnesses. These witnesses agreed in the facts that Patterson and Hughes came into the store together, and, as they came in, Hughes spoke to them, saying that he had a paper that he wished them to sign; that it was Patterson's last will and testament; that Hughes thereupon read the attestation clause in the hearing of Patterson, as well as the witnesses, and then asked Patterson if that was his last will and testament, to which he replied that it was. One of the witnesses further swore that he thought the question was then asked him (the testator) about his signing the will, and the reply of Hughes was, that "he signed it up to my house"; to which Patterson said "Yes." This, however, was not recollected by the other witnesses, and Hughes declared, with a good deal of confidence, that nothing was said in the store about his having signed it.

The Surrogate refused to admit the will to probate, on the ground that the testator had not subscribed the will, or acknowledged the subscription thereto in the presence of the attesting witnesses; but, on appeal, the decree of the Surrogate was reversed, and the court held the acknowledgment was sufficient, because the testator was present and assented when Hughes said he signed it.

The third subdivision of the statute provides that the testator, at the time of making the subscription, or at the time of acknowledging the same, shall declare the instrument so subscribed to be his last will and testament. This safeguard was considered necessary, in view of the fact that persons had been imposed upon, believing they were executing a different paper, when they had been induced to sign a will. Only a few States, however, insist on this formality; besides, New York, California, New Jersey,* and North Carolina require a publication.

There cannot be any uniform, precise mode to make this declaration; it is sufficient if the testator fully and intelligently communicate his knowledge of the instrument being his will to the witnesses; so that he cannot be mistaken as to its nature, and that it shall be so understood by the witnesses.† The minds of the parties must meet; each must understand the particular business he is engaged in. And this mutual knowledge must arise from something said, done, or signified contemporaneously with the execution of the instrument.‡ It will not suffice that the witnesses have elsewhere, and from other sources, learned that the document which they are called to attest is a will; it must be a clear and unequivocal communication of the fact from the testator himself in some manner to them at the time.§

The leading case on this provision of the statute is that of Remsen v. Brinckerhoff, ‖ determined in the court of last resort in 1841. This case arose in the Surrogate's Court in New York, on a proceed-

---

* Den v. Mitton, 7 Halst. 70. † Torrey v. Bowen, 15 Barb. 304.
‡ Lewis v. Lewis, 1 Kern. 222. § 1 Denio, 33.
‖ 26 Wend. 325.

ing to prove the will of Dorothea Brinckerhoff. The will was signed by the testatrix in the presence of two witnesses. The attestation was the usual one signed by the witnesses, showing that the full requirements of the statute were observed. One of the witnesses, on the trial, testified that the testatrix executed the will in his presence by writing her name, and acknowledging it to be her hand and seal for the purpose therein mentioned; that he subscribed in the presence of the testatrix; that the will was not read to the testatrix, nor did he read it; he read the last line of the attestation. Nothing passed between her and him as to its being a will. The other testified that he saw the testatrix sign the instrument. She did not say it was her will; but acknowledged her signature for the purposes therein mentioned. She requested him to sign his name as a witness, and directed him to write his place of residence. He testified further that he never saw the testatrix before that time, and remained in the room only no more than ten or fifteen minutes. On this evidence the Surrogate admitted the will to probate. Some of the heirs and next of kin appealed to the Circuit Judge, who confirmed the decree of the Surrogate. They then appealed to the Chancellor, who reversed the decree of the Surrogate. Finally, the case was taken to the Court of Errors, and the decision of the Chancellor was affirmed, that the instrument was invalid, for want of a declaration, at the time of subscribing or acknowledging the subscription, that the instrument was a will.

A late case, decided in the New York Court of Appeals in 1875, will henceforth be an authority on this point. It was the case of Thompson v. Seastedt.* The case arose on an appeal from the Supreme Court, reversing a decree of the Surrogate of New York City, refusing to admit to probate the will of Eliza Seastedt, on the ground that it was not formally declared by her. It appeared that the will was drawn by direction of the testatrix as her will, and read over to her as such; that she appeared to read it over herself, remarked it would do, and signed her name to it, and procured two of the witnesses to subscribe their names to it. The witness who drew the will testified that he was asked to go to the house to draw it, and was a witness to it, although not directly asked to sign it. The second witness said that he heard the decedent ask the first witness to sign it as a witness; and her husband swore that she asked both of the other witnesses to sign it. The second witness also said that she asked him to witness the signing of her name, and the making of her will, and her husband said she took it after all had signed it, and put it in an envelope. It also appeared that the testatrix signed the will in the presence of the witnesses, and that they signed it in her presence, and in the presence of each other; also, that the wording of the instrument declared it to be her last will and testament, and that she declared it to be such at the time of her subscribing.

The Supreme Court held that the proof as to the

* Not yet reported; may be in 59 N. Y.

execution, witnessing, and publication was sufficient to entitle the will to probate; that, although the testatrix did not, in words, declare the instrument to be her will, she treated it as such, and designed the witnesses to understand it to be such, and that this was equivalent to such a declaration, and was sufficient to satisfy the requirements of the statute. On appeal, the Court of Appeals affirmed this judgment, in an opinion by Folger, J.

This must be deemed a satisfactory and equitable decision, and will have a tendency to check the vexatious and expensive litigation so ruinous to heirs and to an estate, whenever contestants think there was a disregard of the slightest technical requisites in the execution of a will.

The fourth and last requirement of the statute in New York is, that there must be two witnesses who shall sign at the end at the request of the testator. In the majority of our States, only *two* witnesses are required to properly attest a will. There are, as far as we can make out, about ten States that require *three* witnesses. The New England States require three witnesses, and so do Florida, Georgia, Maryland, South Carolina, and Mississippi, but in the last only one witness is required for a will of personal property.

It is observed that the New York statute does not in terms require the witnesses to sign in the presence of the testator or in the presence of each other, as the most of our States do: as, for instance, California, Connecticut, Georgia, Massachusetts, and many others. The former statute in the State required a signing *in the presence of the testator*, but these words having been omitted from the Revised Statutes, it has been decided in two adjudicated cases that it is not necessary that the attesting witnesses should sign their names in the presence of the testator in the strict sense of the requirement of the former law.* In Ruddon v. McDonald, the testatrix subscribed the will in a small bedroom, and the witnesses signed in an adjoining room. The door between the two rooms was open, but the place where the witnesses signed was in a part of the room where the testatrix could not see the witnesses signing without putting her head down to the foot of the bed, if she could then; and they did not look to be able to say whether they could see her face at the time or not. In such States as require a signing in the presence of the testator these wills would not be entitled to probate. Even in these States, a strict literal compliance is not required; the courts adopt what is termed a doctrine of a constructive presence; which in plain language is just this—if a testator could see, and won't see, he should see, and must be supposed to have seen. There never were finer distinctions made on any matter in law than just on this point; indeed, they are more nice than wise, and hair-splitting was never carried to a finer point. Thus, where a testator lay in a bed in one room, and the witnesses went through a small passage into another room, and there set their names at a table in the middle of the room, and opposite to the

---

* Ruddon v. McDonald, 1 Bradf. 352 ; Lyon v. Smith, 11 Barb. 124.

door, and both that and the door of the room where the testator lay were open, so that he might see them subscribe their names if he would, and though there was no positive proof that he did see them subscribe, yet that was sufficient under the statute, because he might have seen them; it shall therefore be considered in his presence.* But where the attesting witnesses retired from the room where the testator had signed, and subscribed their names in an adjoining room, and the jury found that from one part of the testator's room a person, by inclining himself forward, with his head out at the door, might have seen the witnesses, but that the testator was not in that part of the room, it was held that the will was not duly attested.† It would almost seem, from these and other decisions, that the validity of the act depended upon the range of the organs of sight of the devisor, or upon the agility of his movements; whether he were able to turn his body to the foot of the bed, or stretch his neck out of the door.

In Georgia, the testator must have been in such a position as to be able to see the witnesses sign, to constitute presence.‡ And where the witnesses did not sign in the same room where the testator was, it raises a presumption that it was not in his presence; but if the jury find that he might have seen it, and knew it was going on, and approved it, it is good.§

The whole requirements of the statute are gen-

---

* Davy v. Smith, 3 Salk. 395.   † Doe v. Manifold, 1 M. & S. 294.
‡ Reed v. Roberts, 26 Ga. 294.   § Lamb v. Girtman, 26 Ga. 625

erally embodied in an attestation clause which is signed at the end by witnesses. This is no part of the will, and might be omitted without endangering the will, provided the witnesses, whose names are subscribed, can testify as to the observance of the various requirements; but it is unsafe to trust to the memory of witnesses, and almost always the attestation clause is appended. In those States where no subscribing is required, the following is a good form:

"Signed, sealed, published, and declared, by the said A B, the said testator, as and for his last will and testament, in the presence of us, who, in his sight and presence, and at his request, and in the sight and presence of each other, have subscribed our names as witnesses thereto."

The following is suited to the requirements of the Revised Statutes of New York:

"Subscribed and acknowledged by the testator, A B, in the presence of each of us, who have subscribed our names as attesting witnesses thereto at the request of the said testator. And the said testator, A B, at the time of making such subscription and acknowledgment, did declare this instrument so subscribed to be his last will and testament."

A more general form is the following:

"Signed, sealed, published, and declared by the testator, to be his last will and testament, in the presence of us, who, at his request, and in his presence, and in the presence of each other, have subscribed our names as witnesses."

CHAPTER III.

TESTAMENTARY CAPACITY.

As a general rule, this capacity exists; but there are certain conditions which preclude the exercise of this privilege, because of an inability to exercise it either safely, wisely, or intelligently; and these conditions may be, with respect to age, physical or mental incapacity, and coverture.

SECTION 1.—INCAPACITY AS TO AGE.

The age at which a person is permitted to exercise this right varies with the nature of the property, whether it be real or personal property. Under the old common law, a male was qualified to make a will of personal property at fourteen, and a female at twelve;* and this was the rule in England until 1838.† This was the rule of the Roman law; but now it is changed by statute both in England and in this country. In New York, males require to be of the age of eighteen, and females of the age of sixteen, before they can make a will of personal property.‡

In many of our States, the same age is required

---

* Black. II, 497. † Redfield on Wills, I, 15.
‡ 2 Rev. Stat. 60.

for making a will of personal as for real property; and as a general rule, the age required is twenty-one; but in three of our States, California, Connecticut, and Nevada, a person of the age of eighteen is qualified to make a will of personal and real estate. In some, a female attains her majority for this purpose earlier than a male person, as in Illinois, Maryland, and Vermont, where a female is qualified at eighteen.

With regard to the reckoning of the period of a person's majority, there is a novel and exceptional mode in law. Thus, if a person be born on the first of February, at eleven o'clock at night, and the last day of January, in the one-and-twentieth year, at one o'clock in the morning, he makes his will and dies, it is a good will, for he, at the time, was of age. This rule, first laid down by Lord Holt,[*] is well established by sound authority.[†] With regard to which, Redfield remarks: "We feel compelled to declare that the rule thus established in computing the age of capacity, seems to us to form a very singular departure, both from all other legal modes of computing time, and equally from the commonly-received notions on the subject."[‡]

Section 2.—Physical or Mental Incapacity.

The physical incapacity of the deaf and dumb formerly disqualified them from making a will. Blackstone lays down the rule:[§] "Such persons as are

---

[*] 1 Salk. 44.
[‡] Wills, I, 20.
[†] Black. I, 463; 2 Kent, 233.
[§] Com. II, 497.

born deaf, blind, and dumb, as they have always wanted the common inlets of understanding, are incapable of having *animum testandi*, and their testaments are therefore void." And in Bacon's Abridgment,* it is said: "A man who is both deaf and dumb, and is so by nature, cannot make a will; but a man who is so by accident may, by writing or signs, make a will." But since this class of persons have, of late, been brought to a considerable intelligence by the humane efforts of worthy men to communicate knowledge to them, there is no longer any reason or sense in excluding them from the testamentary privilege. However, in their cases, greater circumspection is needed in communicating with them as to their intention, and a stricter regard is paid to the observance of the requirements of execution. The question was carefully examined by the Surrogate of New York,† with the following results:

The law does not prohibit deaf, dumb, or blind persons from making a will. Defects of the senses do not incapacitate, if the testator possesses sufficient mind to perform a valid testamentary act. The statute does not require a will to be read to the testator in the presence of the witnesses; but it is proper to do so when the testator is blind and cannot read. In such cases, the evidence must be strong and complete that the mind accompanied the will, and that the testator was in some mode made cognizant of its provisions. This may be

---

* Wills, B.   † Weir v. Fitzgerald, 2 Bradf. 42.

established by the subscribing witnesses, or by other proof.

So, also, it seems a drunken man, who is so excessively drunk that he is deprived of the use of his reason and understanding, cannot make a will during that time; for it is requisite, when the testator makes his will, that he be of sound and perfect memory; that is, that he have a competent memory and understanding to dispose of his estate with reason.*

We come now to treat of that incapacity which gives rise to most frequent and difficult litigation, and upon which judicial discrimination is most generally exercised—the incapacity of those who are of unsound mind, or persons *non compos mentis*.

There is no investigation in the whole domain of law that is attended with so many lamentable phases, where the foibles, indeed, the ludicrous side, of human nature, are more exposed; for it happens that those who will most carefully and tenderly screen a man's weaknesses, vagaries, and eccentricities whilst he is living, will, if a contest takes place in which they are interested, after his death, most readily reveal, in all their nakedness and boldness of outline, the infirmities and superstitions of the deceased.†

As a principle of law of universal application, a person of unsound mind is incompetent to make a

---

* Swinb. Pt. II, Secs. 1 and 6.

† No better illustration of this ever took place than the case of the will of Captain Ward, over whose will a remarkable contest is taking place [1875] in Detroit.

valid disposition of his property, either before or after his decease, except during a lucid interval. The only difficulty is, to determine exactly and unerringly the particular persons who may be thus classed, and to agree upon some mode or standard by which we can class such unfortunate people. Here is the difficulty; for all men do not view a person's acts in the same manner, and are not similarly impressed by them. What, to some, would infallibly be the exhibitions of a diseased mind, may, to others, be the harmless frolics of a person of odd and eccentric manners. And, just for this reason, the decisions of courts have fluctuated, and, on this subject, have been the least satisfactory. When we lay down a definition of insanity, and agree upon it, we are next met with the further difficulty, to bring the facts of a person's life or actions within it, and so to classify them.

What is the definition of a person *non compos mentis?* The law has to depend on medical writers for this information. Taylor, in his Medical Jurisprudence, gives us a definition as follows: "The main character of insanity, in a legal view, is said to be the existence of *delusion; i. e.*, that a person should believe something to exist which does not exist, and that he should act upon this belief." Another definition is this: "Where there is delusion of mind, there is insanity; that is, when persons believe things to exist which exist only, or, at least, in that degree exist only, in their own imagination, and of the non-existence of which neither argument nor proof can convince them: these are of unsound mind."*

The rule of the common law, until within the last hundred years, was, that it required that a person should be absolutely a lunatic, that there should be entire alienation of mind, in order to incapacitate him from making a will; and there was no such theory then as partial insanity, or *monomania*, which the law takes notice of in modern times. The rise and acceptance of this theory mark an epoch in legal adjudications; it is certainly an advance in the science of law in the last century.

The germ of this theory was first broached in the celebrated case of Greenwood.† In that case, Mr. Greenwood, a barrister, whilst insane, took up an idea that his brother had administered poison to him, and this became the prominent feature of his insanity. In a few months he recovered his senses, and was able to attend to his business, but could never divest his mind of the morbid delusion that his brother had attempted to poison him, under the influence of which (so said) he disinherited him.

On a trial in the Court of King's Bench upon an issue *devisavit vel non*, a jury found against the will; but a contrary verdict was had in another court, and the case ended in a compromise. On the theory of the common law, as it then stood, this will being made in a lucid interval should have been valid.‡

* Sir John Nicholl, in Dew v. Clark, 3 Add. 79.
† White v. Wilson, 13 Vesey, 88.
‡ The case of Lucas v. Parsons, 24 Ga. 640, was very similar to this

The case in which the law first sanctioned the view of partial insanity, which is also one of the landmark cases therefore, was the case of Dew v. Clark,* which excited great interest, and received a very thorough examination by one of the ablest judges of modern times, Sir John Nicholl. It was proved that the testator regarded his daughter as invested with singular depravity, a peculiar victim of vice and evil, the special property of Satan from her birth, and in consequence disinherited her. The syllabus of the case presents in so clear and concise manner the pith of the decision, that it will be useful to quote it:

"Partial insanity is good in defeasance of a will founded immediately (so to be presumed) in or upon such partial insanity. If A, then, makes a will, plainly inofficious in respect to B, and *is proved, at the time of making it, to have been under morbid delusion* as to the character and conduct of B, the Court will relieve by pronouncing this will to be invalid, and holding A to have died intestate."

It is from this case, as a starting point, has arisen the theory of monomania, as applied to testamentary capacity. Henceforth a valuable and practicable rule was established, subsequently recognized and enforced in the best considered cases both in England and America—a rule not so much depending on precedent as it does on sound reason and argument. There must be two elements, co-existing, to

---

case of Greenwood. There, the testator's delusion was in respect to his eldest son, whom he disinherited. The will was set aside.
* 3 Add. 75.

afford sufficient ground for pronouncing a will invalid at the instigation of relatives and others, who deem themselves cut off from the bounty of a testator by his monomaniacal delusions.

First. There must be a plainly inofficious will; or a will wanting in natural affection and duty.

Second. There must be morbid delusion actually existing at the time of making, in respect to the persons cut off, or prompting the provisions of the inofficious instrument.

This theory is now consistently followed in the courts of this country, and an examination of a few remarkable and historical cases will illustrate the application.

It is thus adopted as a principle of decision in Seaman's Friend Society v. Hopper,* by Judge Denio: "If a person persistently believes supposed facts, which have no real existence except in his perverted imagination, and against all evidence and probability, and conducts himself, however logically, upon the assumption of their existence, he is, *so far as they are concerned*, under a morbid delusion, and delusion in that sense is insanity. If the deceased, in the present case, was unconsciously laboring under a delusion, as thus defined, in respect to his wife and family connections, who would have naturally been the objects of his testamentary bounty *when he executed* his will, or when he dictated it, and the court can see that its dispository provisions were or might have been caused or affected by the delusions, the instrument is not his will, and cannot

---

* 33 N. Y. 619.

be supported as such in a court of justice." The same was the ruling in Leach v. Leach.*

Still, there needs to be a careful limitation of this theory. If we were to undertake to class all those who exhibit aberrations of conduct in various directions of life, who labor under hallucinations, and a wild imagination in regard to certain matters, whose credulity or whims provoke our mirth as much as our astonishment, as possessing a diseased mind, we should class among such some of the most singularly gifted and acute minds of the world. We all know of numerous cases in which

> "Some one peculiar quality
> Doth so possess a man, that it doth draw
> All his effects, his spirits and his powers
> In their confluxions all to run one way."

Hence we must distinguish between mere eccentricity and monomania. In monomania, a man is not conscious of entertaining opinions different from the mass of men, and refuses to be convinced of laboring, in any degree, under mental unsoundness; the eccentric man is aware of his peculiarity, and persists in his course from choice, and in defiance of the popular sentiment. A remarkable case of eccentricity, as the court determined, bordering very close on monomania, was in the case of Morgan v. Boys,† where the will was upheld, on the ground that there was no satisfactory proof of actual unsoundness of mind. The testator devised his property to a stranger, thus wholly disinheriting the heir, or next of

---

* 11 Penn. L. J. 179. † Taylor, Med. Jur. p. 657.

kin, and directed that his executors should "cause some parts of his bowels to be converted into fiddle strings—that others should be sublimed into smelling salts, and the remainder of his body should be vitrified into lenses for optical purposes." In a letter attached to the will, the testator said: "The world may think this to be done in a spirit of singularity, or whim, but I have a mortal aversion to funeral pomp, and I wish my body to be converted into purposes useful to mankind." The testator was shown to have conducted his affairs with such prudence and ability, that, so far from being imbecile, he had always been regarded by his associates, through life, as a person of indisputable capacity.*

Some wills have been refused probate upon the ground of a disgusting fondness for animals, evinced by the testators during their lives or in the testamentary act. In one case, the testatrix, being a female, unmarried, kept fourteen dogs of both sexes, which were provided with kennels in her drawing-room.†

In another case, a female, who lived by herself, kept a multitude of cats, which were provided with regular meals, and furnished with plates and napkins. This strange fondness for animals, in solitary

---

* Mr. William Kensett, whose will was proved in Doctors' Commons, London, in 1855, left his body to the Directors of the Imperial Gas Company, London, to be placed in one of their retorts, and consumed to ashes; if not, he directed it to be placed in the family grave in St. John's Wood Cemetery, *to assist in poisoning the neighborhood.* Generally the curious wills are home-made, but this of Mr. Kensett was made by a solicitor.

† Taylor, p. 658.

females, is not altogether unusual, and is not to be regarded as any certain indication of insanity.*

We will now refer to three cases with some particularity, originating in the Surrogate's Court in New York, each of which is very curious and instructive, and in which we can perceive the application of the rule regarding monomania.

The first is the case of Thompson v. Quimby.† There were several reasons assigned by the contestants for their attack upon Mr. Thompson's will. Among them was the allegation "that the decedent was laboring under delusions amounting to insanity, and had not a disposing mind during the preparation, or at the time of the execution of the will." The instrument was drawn and executed during his last illness, and but a short time before his death. It was a voluminous document, and in it some provision was made for many of his descendants and kinsfolk, but the bulk of his large estate (about $400,000) was left for charitable or religious purposes.

---

* Redfield on Wills, I, p. 84.

In June, 1828, the London papers recorded the singular will of a testator named Garland, containing the following clause: I bequeath to my monkey, my dear and amusing Jacko, the sum of £10 sterling per annum, to be employed for his sole use and benefit; to my faithful dog Shock, and my well-beloved cat Tib, a pension of £5 sterling; and I desire that, in case of the death of either of the three, the lapsed pension shall pass to the other two, between whom it is to be equally divided. On the death of all three, the sum appropriated to this purpose shall become the property of my daughter Gertrude, to whom I give the preference among my children, because of the large family she has, and the difficulty she finds in bringing them up.—Ill. London News, March 2d, 1874.

† 2 Bradf. 449.

The testimony established that the testator was a believer in many superstitions of a vulgar character, and had held them with great pertinacity for many years. Among other delusions, it was claimed he believed in the black art; that he read and experimented upon the teachings of magic; was familiar with disembodied spirits; that he could work spells by formula or incantation; that he could cure diseases by amulets, or by papers bearing certain cabalistic inscriptions, which were to be worn about the person of the sufferer. He professed to know where Captain Kidd's treasures were secreted at Montauk Point, and actually, in company with another, undertook, by the aid of a divining rod, to locate the exact spot where the riches were buried. The experiment was a failure, because, as he declared, the charm under which he worked was broken by the inopportune remarks of his attendant. On one of these occasions he beheld the apparition of the devil (it seems, he had a belief in that personage) in the shape of a large bull, and spoke of this taurine manifestation of the father of evil with great seriousness. It was also alleged that he claimed to see ghosts; that he believed in the supernatural character and significance of dreams, in the philosopher's stone, in clairvoyance, spiritualism, mesmerism, magic glasses, and that he owned a whistle with which he could get everything he wanted. This, and much more to the same effect, was adduced as testimony to prove the insanity of the testator.

On the other side, it was shown that the testator

was a shrewd and intelligent man of business, clear and firm in his judgments. He was largely engaged in affairs; was connected with moneyed institutions; had succeeded in accumulating wealth by his own efforts; was associated in large and responsible enterprises of commerce, and was a regular attendant at Dr. Spring's Presbyterian church.

While the Surrogate did accredit all that was deposed to, to sustain his insanity, he did arrive at this conclusion: "After making every possible reasonable allowance, I have no doubt that Mr. Thompson's mind was impressed with a sincere belief in many absurd notions. There seems sufficient evidence to show that he believed in mesmerism, clairvoyance, divining and mineral rods, dreams, and spiritual influences. He searched for the supposed deposits of Kidd, and ascribed his failure in two instances to the utterance of certain words by the operator. That he said he saw the devil in the shape of a bull seems to be well established. He believed likewise in the efficacy of cures for rheumatism, and fever and ague." Now, there was nothing whatever to connect any of these aberrations or infatuations of the testator with the provisions of his will, or with any one of them; they did not affect his testamentary disposition of his property; and there could not, therefore, have been a successful impeachment of his will on the ground of monomania, or partial insanity. The Surrogate decreed in favor of the will, and the Supreme Court sustained his decree.

The next case we allude to, to further furnish an

illustration of the rule, is the recent case of the Bonard Will. This case is of the very greatest importance, because it was argued with unusual skill and ability, and the testimony of the medical experts was sifted with a thoroughness and minuteness which elicited much instruction upon the more obscure phenomena of mental disease, and the facts revealed being such as to present very distinctly the question of the testamentary capacity of one who entertained singular tenets of a so-called faith. It will be advisable to state the facts somewhat fully. Louis Bonard, a native of France, died at the city of New York, in the Roman Catholic hospital of St. Vincent, on the 20th day of February, 1871. His life had evidently been an eventful one; for, while the testimony leaves in doubt much, and fails altogether to account for more of his antecedent history, it was known that he had been a traveler and a trader in South and Central America, and that he had been a dealer in sham jewelry; that he came to this country some time prior to the year 1855, and had brought with him money; that he had had losses, but at length became successful, and made investments in real estate, which enabled him to accumulate a fortune amounting, at the time of his death, to about one hundred and fifty thousand dollars. During the period of his residence in New York, he lived as a miser. He preferred the society and companionship of artisans and mechanics. He had no relatives in America nor in Europe, so far as was ascertained at the time of the trial, although it has since transpired that he has kindred in France. He was a man of erratic habits and singular beliefs, the latter of which seemed to intensify as his age advanced. He was a misanthrope; but was possessed of an unbounded affection for the brute creation. The evidence shows that he was a believer in metempsychosis; that he expressed the opinion that there might be an emperor in any animal he beheld; that he remonstrated with a person who suggested it would be humane to kill an injured kitten, because, he averred, there was a human soul in the animal's body. But he was a man dextrous and cunning in mechanical arts. He constructed machines for various purposes; he had mental resources likewise, and was a reader of books. The testimony, fairly viewed, showed that he railed at religion and priests; yet he died in the peace of the Roman Catholic Church, and in full communion.*

There appeared also the fact that Mr. Bonard combined with his ardent love of animals an unbounded admiration for the benevolence of Mr. Henry Bergh. Memoranda were found among his papers which plainly showed he had some ulterior purpose concerning that gentleman. On the 11th of February, 1871, and while he was very ill, he made a will, bequeathing a portion of his property to two of his friends. On the 13th he made another, revoking the former, and left all his estate, real and personal, to the Society for the Prevention of Cruelty to Animals, of which Mr. Bergh was then,

---

*I am indebted to an admirable essay by Edward Patterson, Esq., of the New York Bar, for the full facts in this case.

as now, the honored president. Here was a case, bold in its outlines, and presenting the salient features of a dogma of a heathen creed, constituting the avowed belief of a man who was born and who died in the Catholic faith. The opinion of the learned Surrogate is very able and interesting. He declares that the belief which Mr. Bonard held did not constitute insanity; that "if a court is to ascribe insanity to a man, or a class of men, constituting a sect according to his or their opinion or belief as to a future state, the logical deduction would necessarily be, that a major portion of all mankind, comprised in all other and different sects, were of unsound mind, or monomaniacs on that subject." The learned Surrogate then proceeds to consider the facts of this case, not as presenting one of general insanity, but as one in which the only appearance of unsoundness of mind consisted in the alleged monomania concerning the transmigration of souls. But he adverts to the fact that there was no connection necessarily of this belief with the terms of the will—that there was nothing *in the will* to show that he held the opinions alleged any more than he was impressed with a belief in utter annihilation after death; nor was there any testimony to associate any provision of the will with a belief respecting the future condition of the human soul. These considerations, coupled with the further fact that "the testator had neither wife nor child, father nor mother, nor any known, near, or remote relatives living, or others on whom he was or felt himself under obligation to bestow his property," induced the court to sustain the will and overrule the allegation of mental incapacity.

But let us suppose that, actuated by this belief, so uncommon in the present day, Mr. Bonard, having before his mind the fate of an itinerant cur running around the city, yelled and hooted at by idle lads, or stunned by a policeman's baton, had feared that his soul after death might pass into the body of such a hapless vagrant, and, under the impression of this possible fate, had provided a safe asylum where such unfortunates might find shelter from the pelting storm; and still further, that there were relatives who would appear and contest the will. Then we introduce quite a different and a new element into the consideration of the case.

This would have indicated that the dispository provisions were intended by the testator for his own physical comfort and benefit in another sphere of physical existence, and would have furnished one and the principal element of that quality of unsoundness of mind which the law recognizes as such in cases of disputed wills.

A late case in New York, decided in June, 1875, by the Surrogate, is another illustration. This was the case of the will of Harriet Douglas Cruger, made when the decedent was seventy-nine years of age, and in which she disposed of the bulk of her very large estate to the American Bible Society, and the Board of Foreign Missions of the Presbyterian Church. The history of the lady's life is an eventful and interesting one. Belonging to a family of wealth and standing, possessed of a large private fortune, and endowed by education and training with rare personal and mental accomplishments, she married early in life, and met with disappointment and misfortune; for it was soon followed by a separation, and a law suit which continued for over eight years, between herself and her husband. She had some nephews and nieces, to whom, at one time, she expressed an intention of leaving her property. In the year 1866, she suffered an injury which affected her mind, and then, at times, was undoubtedly a raving, excited lunatic. Her pastor, the Rev. Dr. Paxton, and her physician, Dr. Parker, testify to her condition then as one of undoubted lunacy. She had on her mind a delusion that the devil was bodily present under her bed, and because of this was in the greatest anxiety and terror. She told her pastor of it, and further communicated to him her intention to give, as a means for her soul's salvation, the most of her property to the religious and charitable societies of her church. He very prudently dissuaded her from this, properly instructing her that her salvation could not depend on such an act, and endeavoring to reason her out of her delusion, but to no purpose. In the fall of 1867, a will was prepared by Charles O'Connor, who was deceived as to her condition, giving her property to the societies named. The will was contested, and rejected, according to the established rule, that her insane delusion, acting on her mind at the time, affected the disposition of her property, and her will was clearly the offspring of such a delusion.

In the case of Austen v. Graham,* the testator was a native of England, but had lived in the East, and was familiar with Eastern habits and superstitions, and professed his belief in the Mohammedan religion. He died in England, leaving a will, which, after various legacies, gave the residue to the poor of Constantinople, and also towards erecting a cenotaph in that city, inscribed with his name, and bearing a light continually burning therein. The court pronounced the testator to be of unsound mind, principally upon the ground of this extraordinary bequest, which sounded like folly, together with the wild and extravagant language of the testator, proved by parol. But on appeal it was held that as the insanity attributed to the testator was not monomania, but general insanity, or mental derangement, the proper mode of testing its existence was to review the life, habits, and opinions of the testator, and on such a review there was nothing absurd or unnatural in the bequest, or anything in his conduct at the date of the will indicating derangement, and it was therefore admitted to probate.

Section 3.—Senile Dementia.

The imbecility and feebleness of mind resulting from extreme old age is another cause of testamentary incapacity. Not that the law fixes a limit beyond which it is presumed a testator cannot exercise the testamentary disposition of his property in-

---

*29 Eng. L. and Eq. 38.

telligently; but it takes into account the well known, familiar instances of the loss of a person's memory and mental capacity, owing to the decrepitude of old age, and it accepts evidence in those instances where senile decay is alleged, as to the ability of an aged person to rightly and understandingly make his will. It was said, in a case in the Ecclesiastical Court in England, that "extreme old age raises some doubt of capacity, but only so far as to excite the vigilance of the court." *

But if a man in his old age becomes a very child again in his understanding, and becomes so forgetful that he knows not his own name, he is then no more fit to make his testament than a natural fool, a child, or a lunatic. †

Courts are not disposed to accept every statement regarding the eccentric or weak movements of an old person as incapacitating such a one from making a will; on the contrary, there is every disposition to permit such a one, if not unmistakably enfeebled in intellect, or unduly influenced, to exercise a right that throws around one, at such a period, a dignity and power entitling them to the respectful regards of those who otherwise might not bestow upon them the attention due to the helplessness of old age. Chancellor Kent well expressed this leaning of courts, in the case of Van Alst v. Hunter. ‡ He says: "A man may freely make his testament, how old soever he may be...... It is

* Kinleside v. Harrison, 2 Phillm. 449.
† 1 Wms. Exrs. 36; Potts v. House, 6 Ga. 324.
‡ 5 Johns. Ch. 148.

one of the painful consequences of old age, that it ceases to excite interest, and is apt to be left solitary and neglected. The control which the law still gives to a man over the disposal of his property is one of the most efficient means which he has, in protracted life, to command the attention due to his infirmities. The will of such an aged man ought to be regarded with great tenderness, when it appears not to have been procured by fraudulent acts, but contains those very dispositions which the circumstances of his situation and the course of the natural affections dictated."

In the case of Maverick v. Reynolds,* it appeared that Mrs. Maverick, at the time of making the will offered for proof, was ninety years of age, and the probate was contested on the ground of testamentary incompetency and undue influence. It was shown that though the old lady did not remember the decease of her son and his wife, that she had sufficient intelligence to inquire about a certain one of her houses, its repairs, and the collection of the rent. One witness stated, as instances of her bad memory, that she forgot to pay her a dollar she had borrowed (a defect of memory not confined to old age); that she was in the habit of making statements, and afterwards denying she had made them, (not confined to old age, by any means) and that she would repeat the same questions after they had been answered. As an instance of the popular belief as to the capacity of old age, one witness said: "She had a bad memory; she was like other old peo-

---

* 2 Bradf. 360.

ple eighty years old; we consider them childish." Another witness, a lady, testified: "As long as I can bring my memory to bear, (a considerable time, it appeared) she has been childish. In my opinion, she was childish twenty-five years ago. She would sing childish and foolish songs, and tell foolish stories, which I considered unbecoming for a woman of her years, and the people would all laugh at it. She would talk sometimes of getting married, and would fancy she was making ready to be married." Against all this was the testimony of her pastor, Rev. Dr. Berrian, that her conversation was devout and pertinent, and he considered her a rather remarkable person for her age. Her physician also testified that he never observed any indication of unsound mind.

Surrogate Bradford, in an able opinion, examined the evidence carefully and at length, and came to the conclusion to admit the will to probate. About her levity, he remarks: "It is worthy of remark, that persons attaining great age often possess a large degree of that cheerful and lively manner which characterizes youth, and which probably in them contributes greatly to a green old age, when others, not so old, and possessing less of this sprightliness and vivacity, appear more decrepid and stricken in years."

As a principle of such cases, he announces: " Great age alone does not constitute testamentary disqualification, but, on the contrary, it calls for protection and aid to further its wishes. When a mind capable of acting rationally, and a memory sufficient in essentials, are shown to have existed, and the last will is in consonance with definite and well settled intentions, it is not unreasonable in its provisions, and has been executed with fairness."

Section 4.—Coverture.

The incapacity arising from coverture is to a great extent removed, and is gradually disappearing by remedial legislation, and for this reason it will not be necessary to treat of it at much length.

There has been a tendency, for many years past, to remove the various property disabilities attaching to a married woman, and which were only to be justified, if then at all, by quite a different state of social organization from the present. Perhaps in no branch of the law have there been so many radical changes as in that part pertaining to the status of a married woman. A lawyer who had only in his mind the old common-law theory and rules, and had neglected to make himself familiar with modern legislation on this subject, would find himself strangely bewildered to define a married woman's rights and powers at the present time.

Still, testamentary power did not come as soon as other rights. Even when the right to a separate and independent ownership of property was granted, the right to a testamentary disposition did not accompany it; as, for instance, in the State of New York, the right to retain for her own use any personal or real property coming to her during marriage, free from any control of the husband, was granted in 1848, but it was not until the next year she was empowered to dispose of it by will.

Married women were excepted from the Statute of Wills of the reign of Henry VIII, which first allowed the disposition of real estate by will in England; but they frequently exercised testamentary disposition under a power given them when an estate was conferred upon them to their separate use.*

They had what was called a *power of appointment* by will, given by the donor of the estate, who was presumed to make the will through them as an instrument.

They could only make a will of personal property by the consent of the husband under the old law,† and this is the case yet in a few States. In Massachusetts, a married woman can dispose of only half of her personal property by will without the consent of her husband; ‡ and some such restriction exists in many of our States.

The law of the American States in regard to the separate estate of the wife being exclusively under her control, and subject to any disposition on her part, is fast verging towards the rules of the Roman civil law, which allowed a married woman the same testamentary capacity, in all respects, as a *feme sole*. § In most of the more important and commercial States, the wife's right to dispose of her estate by will, both real and personal, is recognized

---

* 2 Kent 175. ‡ Gen. Stat., 1855.
† Tucker v. Inman, 4 M. & G. 1049. § Black. II, 497.

to the fullest extent by statute.* The only general restriction is, that she cannot defeat, in her will of her real estate, her husband's right of curtesy. In some States, where the estates by dower and curtesy are abolished, this restriction, of course, cannot exist, as, for instance, in California.

In New York, the power to dispose of her separate real estate by will seems to be unrestricted, for there is no limitation mentioned. But opinions differ on this question: some hold that the husband's right of curtesy is not cut off by the statute, while others hold that the whole unrestricted disposition of her property is given, and that she can defeat her husband's curtesy, even if issue be born and the estate become vested. The matter is in a little uncertainty, because we have not as yet an authoritative opinion of the highest court on the subject, since the remedial statutes were passed. We are inclined to think, however, that the wife can defeat her husband's right of curtesy by a disposition of her estate by will.†

It would be impracticable to give the various statutes of the States on this subject, and, besides, it would be useless, as the changes are very frequent, and what would be correct for a State to-day may to-morrow be obsolete; we have only endeavored to give some general information on the subject.

* Redfield on Wills, 1, 26. † 2 Lans. (N. Y.) 21

CHAPTER IV.

LEGACIES.

People generally understand quite well what is meant by a legacy in a will; but there is a popular meaning attached to the word, which differs from the strict legal meaning. Popularly, we suppose a legacy to be anything — property of any kind, whether real or personal—left to a person in a will; whereas, the strict legal meaning is, that it is a gift of money, or some particular thing, left to a person in a will. When real estate is given, we then term it a *devise*, in a legal point of view; but the word *bequest* is a more general term, as it may designate either a legacy or a devise.

In this chapter, we shall treat of legacies: 1. *As to their Quality;* 2. *Vested or Contingent;* 3. *Conditional;* 4. *Payment;* and 5. *The Person who may take.*

Section 1.—As to their Quality.

Of legacies, there are two kinds—a general legacy, and a specific legacy; with the former is classed what is termed a pecuniary legacy. A legacy is general when it is so given as not to amount to the giving of some particular thing, or money, belonging to the testator. A legacy is specific when it is a bequest of a specified part of the testator's personal estate, which may be distinguished from all others of the same kind. Thus, for example, "I give a diamond ring" is a general legacy, which may be satisfied by the delivery of any ring of that kind; while "I give the diamond ring presented to me by A" is a specific legacy, which can only be fulfilled by the delivery of the identical ring mentioned; for the object is accurately referred to and described, and the legacy can only be satisfied by a delivery in *specie.**

Again, if the testator have many brooches and horses, and bequeath " a brooch" or " a horse " to B, in these cases it is a general legacy; for it is uncertain, from the description, whether any *particular* brooch or horse was intended; so that the bequest may be satisfied by the delivery of something of the same species as that mentioned.† But a bequest "of such part of my stock of horses as A shall select, to be fairly appraised, to the value of $800," or " of all the horses which I may have in my stable at the time of my death," is specific.‡

A bequest to a wife in the following words: "I give and bequeath to my wife, A, the annual sum of £300 sterling each and every year during her natural life, in order that she may live in quiet and easy circumstances," and which, with other legacies afterwards given to her, was expressed to be in lieu of dower, was held to be specific.

If there be an error in the description of the chattel intended to be specifically given, the mis-

---

* Toucht. 433   † 1 Atk. 417.   ‡ Richards v. Richards, 9 Price 219.

take may be of such a nature as not to permit a failure of the specific bequest. If, therefore, A, having *one* horse only, which is white, bequeath it to B by the words "my *black* horse," the mistake is obvious and easily remedied, and the legatee will be entitled to the specific horse, although it be not of the color described; for there can be no doubt of that being the horse *intended* for him, and the legacy will be specific.* If the testator had *two* white horses of different values, and, intending one of them in particular for B, bequeathed it to him by the words, "my white horse," it is presumed that evidence is admissible to show which of the two horses was intended.†

As respects the doctrine of specific bequests, the intention of testators upon this subject, as in every question of the construction of wills, is the principal object to be ascertained; and it is, therefore, necessary that the intention be either expressed in reference to the thing bequeathed, or otherwise clearly appear from the will. The intention must be clear, and courts in general are averse to construing legacies to be specific. ‡

With respect to legacies for money, securities for money, debts, etc., under some circumstances even pecuniary legacies are held to be specific, as of a certain sum of money in a certain bag or chest; § or of £200, the balance due the testator from his

---
* Toucht. 433.
† Selwood v. Mildmay, 3 Ves. 306; 1 Bro. C. C. 477.
‡ Ellis v. Walker, Amb. 310; Kirby v. Potter, 4 Ves. 748; Tifft v. Porter, 8 N. Y. 516.
§ 1 Atk. 508.

partner on the last settlement between them;* but a legacy of "£400 to be paid to A," in cash, is a general legacy.†

Stock or government securities, or shares in public companies, may be specifically bequeathed, where, to use the expression often applied, there is a clear reference to the "corpus" of the fund. Thus, the word "my," preceding the word stock or annuities, has been several times adjudged sufficient to render the legacy specific; as where the bequest is of "*my* capital stock of £1,000 in the India Company's stock." ‡ So a bequest of all the testator's right, interest, and property in thirty shares of the Bank of the United States of America is a specific legacy.§

The distinction between these two sorts of legacies is of the greatest importance; for, in the settlement of an estate by executors or administrators, articles not specifically bequeathed are first to be sold to pay debts and other legacies; and, if there be a deficiency to pay debts, the general or pecuniary legatees have first to abate ratably, or contribute in proportion to the value of their individual legacies. ‖ The principle on which this is done is, the presumed intention of the testator to give a preference to those legatees, by severing particular parts of his personal estate from the rest. But another distinction between them is, that, if the particular thing bequeathed happens, during the lifetime of the testator, to become extinguished, or in some

---

* 3 Bro. C. C. 416.   ‡ Barton v. Cooke, 5 Ves. 461.
† Richards v. Richards, 9 Price, 226. § Walton v. Walton, 7 Johns. 258.
‖ 2 Ves. Sen. 561.

way disposed of by him, which, in law, is called an *ademption*, the legacy fails, which cannot be the case with a general legacy; so that, though specific legacies have, in some respects, the advantage of those that are general, yet, in other respects, they are distinguished from them to their disadvantage.*

The bequest of all a man's personal estate generally is not specific; the very terms of such a disposition demonstrate its generality.† But if a man, having personal property at A and elsewhere, bequeath all his personal estate *at* A to a particular person, the legacy is specific; and, if there is a deficiency of assets to pay other legacies, such a legatee shall not be obliged to abate with the other legatees. ‡ So, where the testator bequeaths the residue of all his personal estate *in the Island of Jamaica*, this is a specific legacy. §

It has been held in Pennsylvania that a pecuniary legacy may be exempt from abatement, as in the case of a wife or child destitute of other provision, or where a legacy is given in lieu of dower. ‖

SECTION 2.—LEGACIES VESTED OR CONTINGENT.

A legacy is said to be *vested* when the right to it, either in the present or in the future, is absolutely given to a person, and does not depend upon the happening of some event. It is *contingent*, if the payment of it is dependent upon the happening of

---

* Wms. Exrs. 994. ‡ Sayer v. Sayer, 2 Vern. 688.
† 1 Roper, 215. § 5 Ves. 150.
‖ Duncan v. Alt, 3 Penn. 383.

some event; as, if a person shall marry, or attain a certain age. The cases establish the principle that contingent or executory interests, though they do not vest in possession, may vest in right, so as to be transmissible to the executors or the administrators of the party dying before the contingency on which they depend takes effect; but where that contingency is the endurance of life of the party till a particular period, the interest will obviously be altogether extinguished by his death before that period.*

The general principle as to the lapse of legacies by the death of the legatee may be stated to be, that if the legatee die before the testator's decease, or before any other condition precedent to the vesting of the legacy is performed, the legacy lapses, and is not payable to the executors or the administrators of the legatee.† But this general rule may be controlled by the manifest intention of the testator appearing upon the face of the will, that the legacy shall not lapse, and by his distinctly providing a substitute for the legatee dying in his lifetime.

The authorities appear to have settled that a testator may, if he thinks fit, prevent a legacy from lapsing; though, in order to effect this object, he must declare, either expressly or in terms from which his intention can with sufficient clearness be collected, what person or persons he intends to substitute for the legatee dying in his lifetime.

In ascertaining the intention of the testator, in

---

* Wms. Exrs. 759. † Idem. 1035.

this respect, the courts of equity have established two positive rules of construction: 1. That a bequest to a person *payable*, or *to be paid*, at or when he shall attain twenty-one years of age, or at the end of any other certain determinate time, confers on him a vested interest immediately on the testator's death, as *debitum in præsenti solvendum in futuro*, and transmissible to his executors or administrators; for the words *payable*, or *to be paid*, are supposed to disannex the time from the gift of the legacy, so as to leave the gift immediate, in the same manner, in respect to its vesting, as if the bequest stood singly, and contained no mention of time. 2. That if the words *payable*, or *to be paid*, are omitted, and the legacies are given *at* twenty-one, or *if*, *when*, *in case*, or *provided*, the legatees attain twenty-one, or any other future definite time, and make the legatee's right to depend on his being alive at the time fixed for its payment, consequently, if the legatee happens to die before that period arrives, his personal representatives will not be entitled to the legacy.*

The application of this rule was well illustrated in the case of Patterson v. Ellis,† and the doctrine discussed and maintained in an opinion by Chief Justice Savage, in the Court of Errors, in New York. It was there held, that where the gift of a legacy is absolute, and the time of payment only postponed, as where the sum of $1,000 is given to A, to be paid when he shall attain the age of twen-

---

* Bacon's Ab. Leg. (E); 2 Vent. 342; Moore v. Smith, 9 Watts, 403.
† 11 Wend. 259.

ty-one, the *time* not being of the substance of the gift postpones the payment, but not the vesting of the legacy; and if the legatee die before the period specified, his representatives are entitled to the money. But where the legacy is given *when* the legatee shall attain the age of twenty-one, or *provided* he attains that age, time is of the substance of the gift, and the legacy does not vest until the contingency happens.

But even where the legacy is given *when* the legatee attains the age of twenty-one, if the devisor directs the *interest* of the legacy to be applied, in the meantime, for the benefit of the legatee, there being an absolute gift of the *interest*, the principal will be deemed to have vested.* The giving of interest before the payment has been considered as evidence of an intention to vest the legacy. Hence, when a portion was devised to a child with interest, but not to be paid or payable until the child should attain twenty-one years, or be married, and the child died under twenty-one, and unmarried, it was decreed that the portion should go to the administrator of the child.†

The rule with respect to the vesting of legacies payable out of real estate is somewhat different. It is this: Where the gift is immediate, but payment

---

* 2 Vern. 673; Van Wyck v. Bloodgood, 1 Bradf. 154.

† Collins v. Metcalfe, 1 Vern. 432. To avoid the lapse of a legacy by the death of the legatee during the lifetime of the testator, the following States have provided against it, if any issue of the legatee be living at the death of the testator: Pennsylvania, South Carolina, Virginia, Maryland, Massachusetts, Connecticut, Vermont, New Jersey, Mississippi, Maine, Rhode Island. (4 Kent, 542.)

is postponed until the legatee attains the age of twenty-one years, or marries, there *it is contingent, and will fail if the legatee dies before the time* of payment arrives; but where the payment is postponed in regard to the convenience of the person, and the circumstances of the estate charged with the legacy—and not on account of the age, condition, or circumstances of the legatee—in such a case it will be vested, and must be paid, although the legatee should die before the time of payment.*

The rule in question is always liable to the operation of the more general and powerful rule, namely, that the intention of the testator, to be gathered from the words of the will, must prevail.

As an illustration of the rule in regard to the vesting of legacies on personal estate, the following is in point: A testator bequeathed to his daughters the sum of £3,000, five per cent. navy annuities, and all the dividends and proceeds arising therefrom, to be equally divided between them, and all his estate at S, to be equally divided between them *when they should arrive at twenty-four years of age*. One of his daughters died before she attained the age of twenty-four years. The court was of opinion that, according to the true rule of construction, the word *when* could not be otherwise considered than as denoting the *period of payment*, and must not be deemed as a condition precedent upon which the legacy was to vest, but merely postponing the payment of this £3,000, with the dividends thereon, till twenty-four.†

---

* 1 Roper, 216; 1 Paige, 33; Harris v. Fly, 7 Paige, 429; Sweet v. Chase 2 N. Y. 73.

† May v. Wood, 3 Bro. 471.

A legacy of £30 was given to an infant to bind him an apprentice. The infant died before he attained a proper age to be bound an apprentice. It was decreed that this legacy was vested, and the infant being seventeen years old, and having made a will, and named an executor, it was allowed to be a good disposition of the £30.*

As to charging legacies on real estate, and observing the rule above laid down, the following is in point:

T S, by will, gave his daughter £1,000, to be paid by his executor at her age of twenty-one, or marriage, which should first happen, willing the same to be raised out of the rents and profits of the lands; and further willed, that in case his son should die before the age of twenty-one, or without heirs of his body lawfully begotten, then from and after the death of his son, he gave all his said lands, etc., to the defendant, he making up his daughter's portion to £2,000; and the daughter died soon after the testator's death, an infant, unmarried, upon which her mother took out letters of administration and claimed the £2,000; it was decreed that she was not entitled to any part of it, for it appears that the intention of the testator was that it should be for a portion, and it is expressly called a portion in the will; it is no personal legacy, but money to be raised out of the rents and profits of lands, and the payment is expressly to be at twenty-one years, or marriage.†

---

* Barlow v. Grant, 1 Vern. 255.
† Duke of Chandos v. Talbot, 2 P. Wms. 612; Smith v. Smith, 2 Vern. 92.

Section 3.—Conditional Legacies.

By the bestowal of legacies a rare opportunity is offered to testators either to gratify some peculiar desire, or to restrain or control some one who is the beneficiary. It is on the legal principle of *quid pro quo*, a consideration for a consideration. Accordingly, we find that testators, in bestowing their bounty by way of legacies, avail themselves of the opportunity to effect various objects—some to regulate and restrain a wayward, errant child, some to curb the eager readiness of a widow to find a new partner, some to check a child rashly rushing into wedlock, and some to gratify a whim or a prejudice.

The law allows conditions to be annexed to a legacy, provided they are not against public policy or good morals.

A conditional legacy is defined to be a bequest whose existence depends upon the happening or not happening of some uncertain event, by which it is either to take place or be defeated.* No precise form of words is necessary to create conditions in wills; wherever it clearly appears that it was the testator's intent to make a condition, that intent shall be carried into effect.

Conditions are subject to the well-known division, into conditions precedent and conditions subsequent. When a condition is of the former sort, the legatee has no vested interest till the condition

---
* 1 Roper, 645.

is performed; when it is of the latter, the interest of the legatee vests, in the first instance, subject to be divested by the non-performance or breach of the condition.

Whether a condition be precedent or subsequent, that is, whether it must be performed before the legatee can be entitled to an absolute interest in the bequest, or not till after, of course depends upon the words and intention of the testator. But a testator, in making a bequest, may use words of condition, which, however, shall not be construed as such, if it clearly appear that they do not involve the *motive* and *reason* of the bequest.* Any consideration exacted from the beneficiary, or any duty imposed on him, unless it is spread over a very unusual period of time, is a condition precedent. A condition that the beneficiary shall cease to resort to public houses is a condition precedent, and is not void for uncertainty.†

In the case of Tattersall v. Howell,‡ a legacy was given, provided the legatee changed his course of life, and gave up all low company, and frequenting public houses. And Sir William Grant held that this was a condition such as the court could carry into effect, and directed an inquiry whether the legatee had discontinued to frequent public houses, keeping low company, etc.

Had this been a devise of land, it would have been a void condition, as will appear in the next chapter.§

In Dunstan v. Dunstan, the executors were re-

---

* Bacon's Ab. Leg. (F.)   ‡ 2 Meriv. 26.
† 37 Miss. 114.   § Moore v. Moore, 47 Barb. 257.

quired by the will to pay to the legatee annually $200, and also one-fifth of the testator's estate, in case the legatee should refrain from vicious habits, and conduct himself with sobriety and good morals. About two years after the testator's death, the legatee filed his bill against the executors, insisting that he had reformed, and claiming the payment of his share of the estate. The defendants had refused to pay over to the claimant his one-fifth of the estate, not being satisfied of his complete reformation. The provision of the will was supported, and as the complete reformation of the legatee was not distinctly proved, and a sufficient time had not elapsed between the death of the testator and the filing of the bill to enable the executors to form a sound opinion as to the permanency of the legatee's good conduct, it was held that the executors were right in refusing to place the whole property in his hands at that time, and it was referred to a Master to ascertain and report whether there had been such a permanent reformation in his character and habits as to entitle him to receive the whole amount bequeathed to him at that time.

If the condition is at all capable of being construed as subsequent, it will be deemed to be such. Thus, in Page v. Hayward,* lands were devised to A and B in case they married a person named S. They married each a person of a different name, yet they were held to take vested interests, the condition being subsequent, and being capable of being performed, as their husbands might die, and

---

* 2 Salk. 570.

they might then marry persons of the coveted name.

A testator declared that if either Jane or Mary married into the families of Prudence or Resignation, and had a son, then he gave all his estate to such son; but if they did not marry, then the estate was to go to A. Jane and Mary married, but not into the families mentioned, and A claimed the estate; but it was held that during the lives of Jane and Mary the claim was premature, for one of them might afterwards satisfy the condition.*

The race as well as the religious antipathy of a testator sometimes crops out in his will.† The testator in the following instance must have had as much dislike to Scotchmen as the celebrated Dr. Johnson. He devised his real and personal estate to trustees, out of which to pay an annuity to his wife for life, and out of the residue to pay sufficient for the maintenance, education, and support of his only daughter until she should attain the age of twenty-one years, or marry, and then in fee, with a proviso that if either his wife or daughter should marry a Scotchman, then his wife or daughter so marrying should forfeit all benefit under his will, and the estates given should descend to such person or persons as would be entitled under his

---

* Randall v. Payne, 1 Bro. C. C. 55.

† A legacy was sometimes given on condition that the legatee should not marry a Roman Catholic. As late as April, 1869, the Hon. Araminta Monck Ridley, in London, left a clause in her will that "if any or either of my said children, either in my lifetime, or at any time after my decease, *shall marry a Roman Catholic*, or shall join or enter any Ritualistic brotherhood or sisterhood, then in any of the said cases, the several provisions, whether original, substitutive, or accruing, hereby made for the benefit of such child or children, shall cease and determine, and become absolutely void."

will in the same manner as if his wife or daughter were dead. It was held that such partial restraint of marriage was legal, and that, the daughter having while under age married a Scotchman, and died leaving a son, the son could not inherit.*

The most interesting inquiry in connection with conditional legacies, is, as to how far conditions annexed to legacies which restrain marriage are to be performed, and in what case the neglect or non-performance of them will forfeit the legacy. The Roman civil law made absolutely void all such conditions in restraint of marriage, as against the policy of the State; but our law has not evinced the same impatience of nuptial restrictions, for a condition inhibiting marriage until majority, or any other reasonable age, or requiring consent, or restraining marriage with any *particular* individual, and in the case of a widow, even a general restraint, is lawful.†

Thus, if an annuity be bequeathed by a man to his wife for so many years, if she shall remain so long a widow, it is a good conditional bequest, because of the particular interest every husband has in his wife remaining a widow, for thereby she will the better take care of the concerns of his family. ‡ But if a stranger gives a legacy upon such condition, it is not a good condition, for there is no more

---

* Perrin v. Lyon, 9 East. 170.
† Scott v. Tyler, 2 Bro. C. C. 488. This is a leading case, and the arguments of the leading counsel engaged contain much of the law on the subject. See Amb. 209.
‡ Godolp. Leg. 45.

reason restraining a widow from marrying than a maid.*

In the American States, we permit such a condition to be annexed to a legacy, as well as in England.†

A restraint of this sort, annexed as a condition, occurred in a case in Pennsylvania,‡ in connection with the will of William Geigley, and, as a singular instance of a testator's forethought and exactness, together with an unusual effusion of sentimental argument, very seldom met with in the sober, well considered decisions of courts, it will be interesting to refer to it.

The testator provided as follows: " I will and bequeath to my loving wife, Susan Geigley, all my real and personal estate that I am possessed of, (with a few exceptions, that I will afterwards bequeath to my brother George) provided my wife Susan remains a widow during her life. But in case she should marry again, my will is, she then shall leave the premises, and receive all the money and property she had of her own, or that I received of hers. . . . . . It is my will and desire, that if my wife remain a widow during her life on the premises, that after her death all the money or property that I got or had of my wife's shall be paid to her friends, whomsoever she wills it to ; and all property belonging to me as my own at my death (not including my wife's part) I will and bequeath to my father and mother, if living. But if they are

---

* Godolp. 46. †2 Redfield, 295.
‡ Commonwealth v. Stauffer, 10 Penn. 350.

both deceased, my will is that my brother, George Geigley, and my sister, Catharine Geigley, shall have the whole of that share or part that was my own, to them, their heirs and assigns, forever."

This condition was held to be good, and, the widow having married, the mother became entitled to the proceeds of the real estate.

The language of the judge before whom the case was at first heard is deserving of a place in legal literature, as something rare in these matter-of-fact, prosaic days. He thought it shocking to his sense of personal liberty that any such restraint should be valid, and concludes his decision with the following beautiful effusion:

"The principle of reproduction stands next in importance to its elder-born correlative, self-preservation, and is equally a fundamental law of existence. It is the blessing which tempered with mercy the justice of expulsion from Paradise. It was impressed upon the human creation by a beneficent Providence to multiply the images of himself, and thus to promote His own glory and the happiness of His creatures. Not man alone, but the whole animal and vegetable kingdom are under an imperious necessity to obey its mandates. From the lord of the forest to the monster of the deep—from the subtlety of the serpent to the innocence of the dove—from the celastic embrace of the mountain Kalmia to the descending fructification of the lily of the plain, all nature bows submissively to this primeval law. Even the flowers which perfume the air with their fragrance, and decorate the forests and fields with their hues, are but curtains to the nuptial bed. The principles of morality—the policy of the nation—the doctrines of the common law—the law of nature and the law of God—unite in condemning as void the condition attempted to be imposed by this testator upon his widow."

It may be considered an unfair partiality in our law that wives are not allowed the same privilege to prohibit their husbands from marrying again; for it has just been lately decided in England, in the case of Allen v. Jackson,* that while a restraint of a *widow* is a good condition and valid as such, a similar restraint of a *widower* in regard to his marriage is invalid, and of no effect. It would seem at first blush that the same rule should govern in each case; but Vice-Chancellor Wood, in Newton v. Marsden,† suggested a reason which he thinks justifies the distinction, namely, that a condition restraining the marriage of a widow is valid, because it is not an arbitrary prohibition of marriage, but the condition of a gift, made to the widow because she was a widow, and because the circumstances would be entirely changed if she entered into a new relation.‡

---

* L. R. 19 Eq. 631.
† 2 J. and H. 356.
‡ In the following instance, a testator is not content only to have his wife remain a widow—he must have her display the appropriate *insignia* of her situation. Mr. James Robbins, whose will was proved in October, 1864, in London, declares: "That, in the event of my dear wife not complying with my request, *to wear a widow's cap after my decease,* and in the event of her marrying again, that then, and in both cases, the annuity which shall be payable to her out of my estate shall be £20 per annum and not £30." As there was no stipulation as to the time the widow's cap was to be worn, probably Mrs. Robbins found it easy to

While the law sanctions, in this case, the restraint of a second marriage, it does not tolerate a general restraint of a first marriage; as Swinburne says:* "A prohibition of the first marriage is much more odious in law than the second." The utmost privilege it has given in this respect is to permit a restraint as to time, place, or person, as not to marry before twenty-one, not to marry at York, not to marry a papist. Still, the law is not indulgent of such conditions, and in some cases will not permit a forfeiture if the condition is not observed. Thus, if a legacy be given on condition of asking consent to marriage, if the person marries without such consent, he does not lose the legacy. Such a condition is said to be *in terrorem* only—something like an idle threat, to prevent persons exercising an imprudent choice.

In Bellasis v. Ermine,† a suit was brought for £8,000, given to the plaintiff's wife. The defendant pleaded that it was given her provided she married with the consent of A, and, if not, that she should have but £100 per annum; and that she married without the consent of A. It was ordered that the plea be overruled. And the court all declared that this proviso was but *in terrorem*, to make the person careful, and that it would not de-

---

comply with the letter of the request in her husband's will, and yet indulge her own taste in the matter. In contradistinction to this was the will of Mr. Edward Concanen, proved in 1868. He says: "And I do hereby bind my said wife that she do not, after my decease, offend artistic taste, or blazon the sacred feelings of her sweet and gentle nature, by the exhibition of a widow's cap."

* Wills, Pt. 4, Sec. 12.
† 1 Ch. Ca. 22.

feat the portion. But it was said that if the party who gave the portion had limited it to another, in the case of her marriage without the consent of A, there it would have been otherwise. We, in this country, follow the same law.* So long, therefore, as the legacy does not go to another named in the will, in case of a breach of the condition, the legatee will be entitled, notwithstanding a marriage without consent. The reason of this is said to be, that the courts cannot relieve against the forfeiture without doing an injury to the person to whom it is limited over.† Thus, A bequeathed £3,000 to his daughter, the plaintiff Garret's wife, at twenty-one or marriage, and recommended her to the care of S, provided that, if she married without the consent of S, her legacy of £3,000 was to cease, and she was to have but £500, and made the defendant, his son, executor. The plaintiff married the daughter without the consent of S, yet the court decreed her the whole £3,000, with interest from the marriage, and principally because it was not expressly devised over.‡

However, courts do not permit this doctrine of *in terrorem* to apply, in case the marriage is to be with consent *during minority*. In such a case the condition is enforced, as it is deemed a safe and proper one for the protection of youth.

The reason of the application of the doctrine *in terrorem*, is, that if a consent be withheld after a person has attained majority, it may be for a long

---

* Parsons v. Winslow, 6 Mass. 169. † 2 Ves. 265.
‡ Garret v. Pritty, 2 Vern. 293.

period, either from caprice, willfulness, or some other cause, and would practically restrain marriage, which is what the law will not permit.*

If a portion be given on condition that the daughter should never marry, such a condition should be rejected as repugnant to the original institution of mankind.†

So, if a condition be illegal, or contrary to the policy of the law, as, if a legacy be given to a woman if she does not cohabit with her husband and lives apart, such a condition is void, and the legatee is entitled absolutely.‡

---

* The case of Bayeaux v. Bayeaux, 8 Paige, 333, is a curious example of an attempt made by a testator to regulate and control the choice of his children in marriage.

The testator died at the city of Troy, in March, 1839, leaving a widow and three infant children. By his will, made a few months before his death, and evidently without the aid or advice of counsel, he placed the following condition on a legacy to his children:

"I charge upon my children, in every possible case, and under all circumstances, never to make a matrimonial engagement, or bind themselves to any individuals by promise of marriage, without full parental approbation and consent as it regards the favored individual. And while I consider it unjust as well as unwise for a parent to coerce, or to attempt forcibly to induce a child to marry an object it cannot love, so do I also deem it without any possible excuse on the part of the child to marry without the full consent of the parents. And in the event of disobedience on the part of my child, in this respect, my wish, desire, and intention is to cut that child off from any participation of the benefits arising from any property I may leave at my decease, of every kind and description whatever."

The provisions of the will were in many respects so vague and indefinite, that Chancellor Walworth remarked: "It is very evident that this will was drawn by the decedent himself, or by some other person equally ignorant, not only of legal language, but of legal principles." He held that the children took the same shares as if their father died intestate.

† Lord Comyns' Rep. 728.
‡ Brown v. Peck, 1 Eden. 140.

Section 4.—Payment of Legacies.

Attention is now to be given to the payment of legacies. It is evident that an executor cannot safely pay a legacy until he ascertains that the personal estate of the deceased is sufficient to pay the debts, and for this reason the law generally allows the space of a year to satisfy himself as to the condition of the personal estate.* And should an executor, acting under the impression that the condition of the assets was such as to entitle him to pay a legacy before the end of the year, pay it before, and if, afterwards, a deficiency arises, he is responsible for the payment of any claim or demand against the estate. Sometimes the exigencies of a person may require an earlier payment of a legacy, and in this case an executor may pay such legacy, provided he gets a bond, with two good sureties, to refund in case of any deficiency; this is the case by statute in New York,† and in many other States. Even if a testator desires a payment of a legacy before the expiration of a year, an executor is not bound to make payment.‡ As regards the time of payment, the law makes no difference between general or specific legacies.

The next inquiry may be as to when a legacy is to be paid, where a legatee is to become entitled at twenty-one, or at some other age, and dies, having a vested interest, before he attains the specified age.

---

*10 Ves. 13. This was the time allowed in the civil law, 2 Salk. 415.
† 2 Rev. Stat. 90.
‡ Benson v. Maude, 6 Madd. 15.

In this case, it is a rule that no payment is to be made until the time arrives when the deceased, if living, would become entitled.* But if interest be given during minority, the representative of the deceased may claim the legacy immediately.†

A legacy of £500 was given to the eldest son of A to be begotten, to place him out apprentice; A had a son born after the death of the testator; and on a bill brought by him for the legacy, it was decreed to be paid, though it was before the time when he was fit to be placed out an apprentice.‡ The following case brings up a reminiscence of a state of society that is now very unfamiliar to us at the present day:

The testator by his will emancipated his slave, and devised to him two hundred dollars, "to assist him in buying his wife." The specification of the object of the bequest does not qualify it, nor affect the legatee's right to it. The executors, it was decided, cannot compel him to use the two hundred dollars in the matrimonial market, nor delay him payment until he makes a purchase there.§

A testator devised as follows: "I lend to my wife the plantation whereon I now live, and after her decease I give and bequeath the said land to my child that my wife is now pregnant with, if a boy; and if it should be a girl, I give the said land to my son H, upon his paying to the said child, if a girl, one hundred pounds." The child proved to

---
* 2 Vern. 31. Roden v. Smith, Amb. 588.
† Cricket v. Dolby, 3 Ves. 13.
‡ Nevil v. Nevil, 2 Vern. 431.
§ Joe v. Hart's Executors, 2 J. J. Marsh. 351.

be a girl; and it was held that the legacy of one hundred pounds was not payable until the death of the testator's widow.*

If a legacy be given to A, with a bequest over if he succeed to a certain estate, or upon condition that it shall be void in that event, the legacy must be paid to A, notwithstanding.†

If a legacy be devised generally, it is regularly to carry interest from the expiration of the first year after the death of the testator; but if it be a specific legacy upon which interest can accrue, the interest will be given from the death of the testator, and it is immaterial whether the enjoyment of the principal is postponed by the testator or not.‡ Even if there be a direction to pay a general legacy as soon as possible, interest only begins at the end of a year.§ But if the legatee, being of full age, neglects to demand it at that time, he cannot have interest but from the time of the demand, because a legacy differs from a debt. ‖

While this was formerly the rule, it is not now in force, for it has been held that, no matter whether the legatee demands or not, the legacy will draw interest. It was so decided in a case in New York.¶

The general rule is, that a legacy payable at a future day does not carry interest before the time of payment; and the rule applies to an infant payable at twenty-one, unless in the case of an infant having a right to demand maintenance from the testator, or of the legacy to him being a residue, or

---

* 1 Hawks 241.
† Fawkes v. Gray, 18 Ves. 131.
‡ Wms. Exrs. 1221; 2 Bradf. 77.
§ 8 Ves. 410.
‖ Poph. 104.
¶ Marsh v. Hague, 1 Edw Ch. 174.

there are special circumstances showing clearly an intention to give interest.* And if a legacy is given in lieu of dower, or is decreed to be a satisfaction of a debt, the court always allows interest from the death of the testator.†

A legacy to a child whose support and maintenance is otherwise provided for by the bounty of the testator, like a legacy to a more distant relative, or to a stranger, is not payable and does not draw interest until one year after the death of the testator, where no time of payment is prescribed by the will.‡

An annuity bestowed by will, without mentioning any time of payment, is considered as commencing at the death of the testator, and the first payment as due at the expiration of one year; from which latter period interest may be claimed in cases where it is allowed at all.§

The rule as to interest being reckoned on a specific legacy from the death of the testator was strictly applied in the case of Churchill v. Speake,‖ where a testator made a specific bequest of a mortgage for £1,000 to his wife, and desired her to give the sum of £500 to M C, his grandchild; "but, for the time and manner of doing it, I leave it freely to herself, and as she shall see it best for her"; and the wife exercised this freedom so well as to live twenty years after the testator, and never paid the £500; and the court decreed payment of it to M C, with interest from the testator's death.

---

* Ves. 10.
† Wms. Exrs. 1222.
‡ Williamson v. Williamson, 6 Paige, 298.
§ 5 Binney 475.
‖ 1 Vern. 251.

The inquiry to whom legacies are to be paid is one of great importance to the executor, who must be careful to pay legacies into the hands of those who have authority to receive them. It is a general rule that, where the legatee is an infant, and would be entitled to receive a legacy if he were of age, the executor is not justified in paying it either to the infant, or to the father, or any other relation of the infant, on his account, without the sanction of a court of equity.* And even in the case of a child who has attained majority, payment to the father is not good, unless it be made by the consent of the child, or confirmed by his subsequent ratification. It may happen that an executor has, with the most honorable intentions, paid the legacy to the father of the infant; nevertheless, he will be held liable to pay it over again to the legatee on his coming of age. And although such cases have been attended with many circumstances of hardship to the executor, yet he has been held responsible, on the policy of obviating a practice so dangerous to the interests of infants, and so naturally productive of domestic discord.†

Many of our States regulate the payment of legacies to infants by statute, as in New York, where a legacy of $50 may be paid to the father of the legatee, to the use and for the benefit of such minor; but, if it exceeds $50, it must be paid to the general guardian of the infant, who will be required to file a bond to pay it over to the infant.‡

* 1 Johns. Ch. 3.   † Wms. Exrs. 1206–7.   ‡ 2 Rev. St. 450.

It was formerly the law that, if a legacy was given to a married woman, it should be paid to the husband. So, where a legacy was given to a married woman living separate from her husband, with no maintenance, and the executor paid it to the wife, and took her receipt for it; yet, on a suit instituted by the husband against the executor, he was decreed to pay it over again, with interest.* It was also adjudged that, if the husband and wife were divorced *a mensa et thoro*, and a legacy was left to her, the husband alone could give a proper receipt for it, and consequently to him alone was it payable.†

But now, by statutes in almost all of our States, a married female may take by devise and bequest, and hold to her sole and separate use, real and personal property, or any interest or estate therein, in the same manner, and with the like effect, as if she were unmarried.

Section 5.—The Person who may Take.

The only person generally disqualified to receive a legacy is the witness to a will. The law has thought fit to guard a deceased from all imposition, and it is thought if a person took any beneficial interest under a will to which he was one of the witnesses, he could not be a disinterested person to attest its due execution.

In New York, he is disqualified, if such will cannot be proved without his testimony;‡ and, in a

---

* Palmer v. Trevor, 1 Vern. 261; Toller 320.   † Wms. Exrs. 1213.
‡ 2 Rev. St. 65. So in California: Civil Code 1282.

case on this head, Caw v. Robertson,* where there were *three* witnesses to the will, each of whom took legacies under it, the Surrogate called the first two, whose names appeared first, which were sufficient, and omitted calling the third. It was decided that he only became entitled to the legacy, as the will could be proved without his testimony.

An executor is not disqualified from receiving a legacy; but in his case, it seems, it will not carry interest.†

In wills, legatees are sometimes designated under a general name or class, and a difficulty often arises to determine what individuals shall be included in such a designation. Where a testator uses such general terms, without defining or limiting them, they have a meaning given them by the general rules of construction in law. Indeed, the testator's intention may be frustrated by using certain terms, which may appear to him to include or exclude certain individuals in his bounty, but which may be so enlarged or restricted by the rules of law as to defeat their object. As in the instance where a lady, dying, and intending to give her personal wearing apparel to her servant maid, bequeathed to her *all her personalty*, which under the rules of law meant all her personal estate, which was valued at $60,000, and which under such a term must necessarily go to the servant.

In general, no rule is better settled than that legatees must answer the description and character given them in the will, but it will presently appear,

---

* 1 Seld. 125.   † Morris v. Kent, 2 Edw. Ch. 182; Preston on Leg. 281.

from the cases, that there are many important exceptions to it.

We shall refer to some of these general names or classes, sometimes met with in a will, by which individuals belonging to such classes become entitled to a legacy.

When a testator leaves a legacy to "children,"* it is a general rule, that those within that designation *at the time of the testator's death* become entitled; but if, from the expressions and context of the will, it is ascertained that he intended only those who answered that description *at the date of the instrument*, such intention will be observed.† A court of equity, however, is careful that a liberal construction be placed upon such a term, and always, if possible, will hold that it shall include children in existence at the death of the testator, and especially if the testator stood in *loco parentis* to the legatees.‡

The general rule, it is claimed in Collin v. Collin, § is, that in a will of personal estate the testator is presumed to speak in reference to the time of his death, and not to any previous or subsequent period.

A child in *ventre sa mere*, at the time of the testator's death, is held to be in *esse*, if it is afterwards

---

* The word "children" includes only the immediate legitimate descendants, and not a step-child: Cromer v. Pinckney, 3 Barb. Ch. 466; Mowatt v. Carrow, 7 Paige, 339. Nor does it include grandchildren: Radcliff v. Buckley, 10 Ves. 195; 4 Watts, 82.
† Sherer v. Bishop, 4 Bro. C. C. 55; 2 Ves. 84.
‡ Doe v. Clark, 2 H. Bl. 399; Balm v. Balm, 3 Sim. 492.
§ 1 Barb. Ch. 637; Wms. Exrs. 934.

born alive, and to be equally entitled as those children who were born in the lifetime of the testator.*

If there be a postponement of the division of a legacy given to a class of individuals until a certain time after the testator's death, every one who comes under the description at the time when the distribution is made will be entitled, no matter if he was not in *esse* at the time of the testator's death, unless from the will it be gathered that the testator intended to limit his bounty to those only who were living at the time of his decease.*

And where the legacy in the will indicates a present bequest of a fund which is to be distributed at a period subsequent to the death of the testator, those who are in *esse* at the time of his death will take vested interests in the fund, but subject to open and let in others who may come into being, so as to answer the description and belong to the class at the time appointed for the distribution. Where, however, a fund is bequeathed to children or others as a class, to be divided equally among the persons composing the class, when they arrive at the age of twenty-one, or marriage, only those who shall have been born or begotten when the oldest arrives at the age of twenty-one, or when the first of the class is married, are entitled to share in the fund.*

Although, as a general rule, a devise to children, without any other description, means legitimate

---

* Rawlins v. Rawlins, 2 Cox's Ca. 425; Marsellis v. Thalheimer, 2 Paige, 35.

† Jenkins v. Freyer, 4 Paige, 47.

‡ Collin v. Collin, 1 Barb. Ch. 630.

children, and if the testator has such children, parol evidence cannot be received to show that a different class of persons was intended; still, in these cases, as in all others, it is proper to look into circumstances *dehors* the will, to see whether there are any persons answering the description of the legatees in the legal sense of the term used; and if it appear that there are not any such persons, it is then allowable to prove the situation of the testator's family, to enable the court to ascertain who were intended by the testator as the object of his bounty. Thus, in Gardner v. Heyer,* where the testator died a bachelor, but had for a long time lived and cohabited with M. Smith, by whom he had and left four children, a son and three daughters, who had been by him placed at school and acknowledged as his children, and were generally reputed as such by his friends; and by his will he gave to his son John $10,000, to be paid to him when he arrived at the age of twenty-four, the interest in the meantime to be applied to his maintenance and education; and he also gave to each of his daughters $3,000, payable at the age of twenty-one, and the interest in the meantime to be applied to their education and support; and he directed his executors and trustees to pay $65 to M. Smith, the mother of the children, quarterly, during her life, if she remained single and had no more children; and he devised and bequeathed all the residue of his estate, real and personal, to his executors and trustees, and the survivor of them in fee, in trust,

---

* 2 Paige, 11.

to pay two-thirds of the income thereof to his son John, and one-third to his daughters during their lives, with remainder to their issue; and he gave cross-remainders to the survivors in case any of the children should die without issue; and he also appointed the executors and trustees, guardians of the children during their minority, and earnestly requested that the utmost care should be taken *of their morals and education.* The court declared that there was no doubt as to the legal and equitable rights of the children of M. Smith under the will.

A bequest to an unborn, illegitimate child, the mother being described, is valid, unless the child be pointed out as having a certain father, for then it is void, the bastard being in point of law nobody's child—*filius nullius.**

A bequest by a husband to his "beloved wife," not mentioning her by name, applies exclusively to the individual who answers the description at the date of the will, and is not to be extended to an after taken wife.†

A testator was betrothed to a lady, and by a codicil to his will, after mentioning her name, and alluding to his intended marriage with her, he gave £3,000 *to his wife.* Before the marriage he died, and it was held that the lady was entitled to the legacy.‡

A gift to "my servants," it is thought, will extend

---

* Pratt v. Flamen, 5 Har. & Johns. 10.
† Garrett v. Niblock, 1 R. & M. 629; Lady Lincoln v. Pelham, 10 Ves. 166.
‡ Schloss v. Stiebel, 6 Sim. 1.

to those in testator's service at the date of the will, though they leave it before his death.* Redfield prefers to comprise, by such a phrase, only those who are in the testator's service at the time of his decease, no matter whether they were his servants at the time of his making his will or not.† The best rule would be not to admit those who entered the testator's service recently before his death, nor those who left before that time, but to hold only those entitled who were in his service when the will was made as well as at his death.

Difficulties sometimes arise from the want of explicitness in pointing out a legatee by a testator, and again from a mistake in naming or designating him. The general rule upon the subject is, that when the name or description of the legatee is erroneous, and there is no reasonable doubt as to the person who was intended to be named or described, the mistake will not disappoint the bequest. The error may be rectified and the true intention of the testator ascertained in two ways: 1. By the context of the will; 2. To a certain extent by parol evidence.

1. The mistake may be rectified by the context. Thus an error in the *name* of the legatee may be obviated by the accuracy of his *description:* as where a legacy is given to "my namesake *Thomas*, the second son of my brother," and the testator's brother had no son named Thomas, but his second son is named *William*, there is sufficient certainty in the description to entitle the second son.

---

* 1 Jarman, 306.   † Vol. II, 96.

And again, where the testator bequeathed to his brother, Cormac Connolly, and to his two sisters, Mary and Ann, a certain residue, and afterwards by a codicil bequeathed as follows: "To my nephew, Cormac Connolly, the son of my brother, Cormac Connolly, the sum of five hundred dollars for his ecclesiastical education, which sum is to be taken from what I have bequeathed to my brother Cormac, and to my sisters Mary and Ann." And it appeared the testator never had a brother named Cormac, but that he had a nephew, Cormac, who was the son of his only surviving brother James, who was pursuing classical studies in Ireland with a view to an ecclesiastical education, and who was the only nephew of that name; it was held that the legatee intended by the testator by the name of his brother, Cormac, was the father of his nephew, Cormac, and that his brother James was the person entitled to share in the residuary estate.*

So, an error in the *description* may be obviated by the certainty of the *name ;* as, where a legacy was given to "Charles Millar Standen and Caroline Eliz. Standen, *legitimate* son and daughter of Charles Standen, now residing with a company of players," and it appeared they were *illegitimate* children, their claim was nevertheless supported.†

The mistake may, to a certain extent, be rectified by parol evidence. The admissibility of parol evidence in these cases has given rise to much dis-

---

* Connolly v. Pardon, 1 Paige, 291. In Thomas v. Stevens, 4 Johns. Ch. 607, a legacy to Cornelia Thompson was held a good bequest to Caroline Thompson, it appearing that she was the person intended.

† Standen v. Standen, 2 Ves. Jr. 589.

cussion; it forms one of the exceptions to the general rule, not to admit parol evidence where a will is void for uncertainty. This is treated of under the *seventh proposition* of Wigram on Wills,* in a very exhaustive manner, and the cases fully examined. We will merely here point out when such evidence is admissible and when it is rejected. The rule is thus laid down: Where the object of a testator's bounty, or the subject of disposition, is described in terms which are applicable indifferently to more than one *person* or *thing*, evidence is admissible to prove which of the persons or things so described was intended by the testator.

Thus, when a *blank* is left for the Christian name of the legatee, parol evidence is admissible to supply the omission, as in the case of Price v. Page,† in which the testator bequeathed " to ——— Price, the son of ——— Price, the sum of £100." No person but the plaintiff claimed the legacy, and he produced evidence from which it appeared that he was the son of a niece of the testator; that his father and grandfather's names were Price; that the testator had no other relation of that name, and that he had been before frequently the object of the testator's care; that the testator said he had and would provide for the plaintiff. Upon this evidence, Lord Alvanley determined in favor of the claim.

When the omission consists of the *entire* name of the legatee, parol evidence cannot be admitted to supply the blank; for that would amount to a bequest by oral testimony. Thus, in Winne v. Little-

---

* See Chap. VIII. † 4 Ves. 680.

ton,* A bequeathed all his personal estate to his executor, leaving a blank, and died without naming *any* person executor. The legacy was adjudged to be void. And in Hunt v. Hort,† a woman devised her houses in the city and at Richmond to her niece, dame Margaret Hort, and Richard Baker, her attorney, in trust to sell. She then gave some pictures specifically, and thus proceeded: "My other pictures to become the property of Lady ———." The testatrix then made her niece, Harriet Hunt, her residuary legatee, and appointed Lady Hort and Richard Baker her executors. Lord Thurlow was of opinion that he could not supply the blank by parol evidence, and observed that, where there was only a title given, it was the same as a total blank.

If, however, a legatee be described by initials of his name only, parol evidence may be given to prove his identity. This was done in the case of Abbott v. Massie,‡ where the bequest was: "Pint Silver Mug and all my China to Mrs. G., and £10 for mourning." Mrs. Gregg claimed the legacies, and (the Master having refused to admit testimony) offered to show that she was the person intended. Exception was taken to his ruling, upon which the court declared that he ought to receive evidence to prove who Mrs. G. was.

The principle upon which parol evidence is admitted in these cases is a presumption of possible ignorance in the testator of the Christian name of the legatee, or of his being accustomed to calling a

---

* 2 Cha. Ca. 51.   † 3 Bro. C. C. 311.   ‡ 3 Ves. 148.

person by the name of Mrs. B, a presumption which, being raised upon the face of the will, may be confirmed and explained by extrinsic evidence. Upon this ground, it is consistent with the established doctrine that such evidence is admissible to remove *latent* ambiguities, but cannot be admitted to explain *patent* ambiguities in a will. This is founded on Lord Bacon's well-known maxim: "*Ambiguitas verborum latens verificatione suppletur.*"

CHAPTER V.

LIMITS TO TESTAMENTARY DISPOSITION.

While the law has generally granted the privilege of testamentary disposition, it has not deemed it expedient or politic to give the absolute and unrestricted power, so that a person can make a posthumous disposition of his property in *any* way he thinks proper. For the public welfare, it has seemed judicious to impose certain restrictions on the right exercised by a person in distributing his property after his decease. It is well known that if an uncontrolled, absolute power were given, that individuals would sometimes disregard the claims of those who have a natural right to their bounty, and gratify their pride, their whims, or their vagaries in disposing of their property by will.

The possession of a large amount of property during a man's lifetime gives him such a consciousness of power and authority, that it is difficult to disabuse his mind of the idea that he cannot perpetuate his name, his influence and control, after his death, by distributing and disposing of his property according to his pleasure.

The law is full of instances where men have attempted, by schemes in devising their property, to establish a name and an influence that would abide long after the mind that conceived them had ceased to act or control.

This has been the ambition, we may call it the infirmity, of some great minds; indeed, it seems sometimes a special characteristic of such persons to desire to live thus in the memory of posterity, by some remarkable and striking mode of disposing of their property after their decease, so as to leave some visible token of their influence and prestige, either in an institution or in a family,* either in a charity or a monument.

When properly and judiciously exercised, this desire has led to the foundation of those noble institutions for the relief of the indigent and helpless, for the promotion of knowledge and education, for the development of science and art, and for the furtherance of various benevolent designs, which are the boast and glory of our modern civilization, and which have done so much to foster and advance that civilization.

But at an early period this desire or infirmity was made use of by the clergy, who wielded such vast influence over the dying, to induce testators to dispose of property for enriching churches and monasteries, and various other institutions. So great did the evil become, and so many grievous abuses sprung up, that the public welfare was threatened and endangered, and in consequence of this, a bitter and determined struggle ensued between the civil and spiritual powers, lasting through centuries and giving a peculiar bias to certain legislation. As soon as some means would be devised to check the abuses, and to limit the power of the clergy,

* Vide the case of Shakspeare, Introduction, p. 23.

some new device would be contrived by their ingenuity to evade the rules or nullify a law. The establishment of the law of Uses and Trusts is a good example of these ingenious devices to evade a statute.

The several Statutes of Mortmain had their origin in this effort of the civil power to curb the influence of the spiritual power, and check a dangerous tendency to enrich corporations of a religious or eleemosynary character. These several acts occupy a prominent place in English history, and characterize a very important epoch of that history. Their influence has extended to us, who have gathered experience from the past, and this is plainly evinced in our Statutes of Wills in the different States, which disqualify corporations from taking by devise unless expressly authorized.*

It was found, however, that an indiscriminate prohibition would prevent the foundation of many worthy and useful institutions, which, instead of being a menace, would be a safeguard to the welfare of the State; and hence a distinction arose between such bequests as were for charitable uses, and those for superstitious uses, the latter of which were so obnoxious to the law, and forbidden by it. A superstitious use is thus defined in Bacon's Abridgement.† It is, "where lands, tenements, rents, goods, or chattels are given secured, or ap-

---

* 2 N. Y. Rev. St. 57; Civil Code Cal. 1275. In Indiana, Massachusetts, and Pennsylvania, there is no Mortmain act.

† Charitable Uses (D). The doctrine of Superstitious Uses cannot be to much extent applicable here, as we have no religion recognized and established by the State.

pointed for and towards the maintenance of a priest and chaplain to say mass; for the maintenance of a priest or other man, to pray for the soul of any dead man, in such a church, or elsewhere; to have and maintain perpetual obits, lamps, torches, etc.,* to be used at certain times, to help to save the souls of men out of purgatory; these and such like uses are declared to be superstitious."

Devises to charitable uses were supported in England at an early period in the common law, which is supposed to have derived its maxims on this head from the civil law. Lord Nottingham says, in the case of the Attorney-General v. Tancred,† that devises to corporations, though void under the Statute of Wills, were good in equity *if given* to charitable uses.‡

The Statute of the 43d of Elizabeth enumerates what charitable uses were. They were, according to this statute, gifts for the relief of aged, impotent, and poor people; for maintenance of sick and maimed soldiers and mariners; for ease of poor inhabitants concerning payment of taxes; for aid of young tradesmen, handicraftsmen, and persons decayed; for relief, stock, and maintenance of houses of correction; for marriages of poor maids;§ for

---

* Vide Will of Lady Alice West, p. 18.
† Ch. Prec. 272. Eyre v. Countess of Salisbury, 2 P. Wms. 119.
‡ Lord Hardwicke, in Jones v. Williams, Amb. 651, defines a charitable use as " a gift to a general public use, which extends to the poor as well as the rich."
§ It may be thought a singular purpose of charity to provide for the " marriages of poor maids," and one that would accomplish but little in a field where the objects would be so numerous; nevertheless, the be-

education and preferment of orphans; for schools of learning, free schools, and scholars in universities; for relief or redemption of prisoners or captives; for repair of bridges, ports, havens, causeways, churches, sea-banks, and highways.

nevolent designs of men have been turned in that channel, as well as in other various directions mentioned in the statute.

By the will of Mr. Henry Raine, a wealthy London brewer, a fund was established for just such a purpose. Among the notable charitable institutions of London, there is none more novel in inception or more unique in management than Raine's Asylum, established by him in 1736, for clothing, educating, and properly training for domestic service forty young girls, taken from a lower school previously established by him. On arriving at the age of twenty-two, any girl who has been educated in the asylum, and who can produce satisfactory testimonials of her conduct while in service, may become a candidate for a marriage portion of one hundred pounds, for which six girls are allowed to draw twice in each year, on the first of May and the fifth of November. The drawing is in this manner: The treasurer, in compliance with the explicit directions of Mr. Raine, takes a half sheet of white paper and writes thereon the words, "one hundred pounds." Next, he takes as many blank sheets as, with the one written on, will correspond with the number of candidates present. Each of these half sheets is wrapped tightly round a little roller of wood, tied with a narrow green ribbon, the knot of which is firmly sealed. The rolls are then formally deposited in a large canister placed upon a small table in the middle of the room. This being done, the candidates, one at a time, advance towards the canister, each drawing therefrom one of the small rolls. When all have drawn, they proceed to the chairwoman, who cuts the ribbon which secures each roll, and bids the candidates unfold the various papers. There is no need to ask which of them has gained the prize—the sparkling eyes of the fortunate "hundred-pound girl" reveal the secret more quickly than it could be spoken by the lips. The scene seems to be one in which Mr. Raine took deep interest, for in his will, after appointing his nephews to purchase £4,000 stock in order to make a permanent provision for these marriage portions, he says: "I doubt not but my nephews would cheerfully purchase the said stock if they had seen, as I have, six poor innocent maidens come trembling to draw the prize, and the fortunate maid that got it, burst out in tears with excess of joy." The portion drawn in May is given after a wedding on the fifth of November; the November portion being given in like manner on May day. The author witnessed one of these marriage ceremonies in the church of St. George's-in-the-East.

The number of marriage portions given since the opening of the asylum is said to exceed three hundred.

But as it was found that persons "dying and languishing"—*in extremis*—were frequently unduly influenced to dispose of their property to such charitable purposes, against the rights of their family or kindred, it was enacted by the Statute of Mortmain, 9 George II, that no property in land, or arising out of land, could pass to such purposes, unless by deed indented, sealed, and delivered in the presence of two or more credible witnesses, twelve calendar months before the death of the donor or grantor.* Of course, these statutes have no operation in this country, unless by special enactment. The statute of Elizabeth not being in force in New York, it was therefore insisted that no devise to charitable uses was, in consequence, valid.

The fluctuations of the law on this point present a remarkable and not a very satisfactory example of varying judicial opinion in that State. The earlier decisions of its highest court have lately been overruled, and the earlier doctrines on the subject discarded. Thus, in Williams v. Williams,† it was held that the law of charitable uses was not founded on the statute of Elizabeth, but was a part of the common law, which is still in force here, so far as conformable to our polity and adapted to our institutions; and that a court of equity, exercising the chancery jurisdiction of the English courts, will carry out the purpose of a testator; and that, not-

---

* This statute has been adopted in Massachusetts, North Carolina, Kentucky, Indiana, Pennsylvania, and several other States. 2 Kent 285. In Pennsylvania, the will, to make a valid devise to charitable uses, must be made a month before the testatator's decease. Price v. Maxwell, 28 Penn. 23.

† 8 N. Y. 525.

withstanding the statutory prohibition against devises of lands to corporations, a devise of a charity, not directly to a corporation, but in trust for a charitable corporation, would be good. Subsequent cases followed this decision of Williams v. Williams; but later cases have altered the law in New York. The case which effected a change, and finally determined the law, is of historical as well as legal importance, and deserves a detailed statement.

It is the case of Levy v. Levy,* most learnedly and ably argued and examined in the various courts of the State. Commodore Uriah P. Levy, the testator, was an eminent and wealthy officer of the United States navy, of the Jewish religion, who became the owner of the famous farm of Jefferson, at Monticello, in Virginia, and who died in New York in March, 1862, leaving property valued at over half a million dollars. In his will, after making various bequests, he provided:

"After paying the above legacies and bequests, or investing for the same, and subject to my wife's dower and use of furniture, I give, devise, and bequeath my farm and estate at Monticello, in Virginia, formerly belonging to President Thomas Jefferson, together with all the rest and residue of my estate, real, personal, or mixed, not hereby disposed of, wherever or however situated, to the people of the United States, or such persons as Congress shall appoint to receive it, and especially all my real estate in the city of New York, in trust, for the sole and only purpose of establishing and maintain-

---

* 33 N. Y. 97, reversing 40 Barb. 585.

ing at said farm of Monticello, in Virginia, an agricultural school, for the purpose of educating as practical farmers, children of the warrant officers of the United States navy whose fathers are dead. Said children are to be educated in a plain way in the ordinary elementary branches to fit them for agricultural life, and to be supported by this fund, from the age of twelve to sixteen, and each of them to be brought up to do all the usual work done on a farm; the said farm to be so cultivated by the said boys and their instructors as to raise all they may require to feed themselves, and the schoolmaster and one other teacher, and one superintendent of the said farm. I also give and bequeath, for the purpose of giving such fuel and fencing for said Monticello farm-school, two hundred acres of woodland of my Washington Farm, called the Bank Farm, in Virginia, the said two hundred acres to be taken from said farm hereby devised to my nephew Ashel, and to be designated by said Ashel.

"In establishing said farm-school, I especially require that no professorships be established in said school, or professors employed in the institution; my intention in establishing this school is charity and usefulness, and not for the purpose of pomp. In proportion to the smallness of number of the teachers, so will industry prevail.

"The institution must be kept within the revenue derived from this endowment; and under no circumstances can any part of the real or personal estate hereby devised be disposed of, but the rent and income of all said estate, real and personal, is to be held forever inviolate, for the purpose of sustaining this institution. The estate and lands in New York can be leased to great advantage for that purpose.

"Should the Congress of the United States refuse to accept of this bequest, or refuse to take the necessary steps to carry out this intention, I then devise and bequeath all the property hereby devised to the people of the State of Virginia, instead of the people of the United States. Provided they, by acts of their legislature, accept and carry it out as herein directed. And should the people of Virginia, by neglect of their legislature, decline to accept this said bequest, I then devise and bequeath all of my said property to the Portuguese Hebrew Congregation of the city of New York, the Old Portuguese Hebrew Congregation in Philadelphia, and the Portuguese Hebrew Congregation of Richmond, Virginia: provided, they procure the necessary legislation to entitle them to hold said estate, and to establish an agricultural school at said Monticello for the children of said societies who are between the ages of twelve and sixteen years, and whose fathers are dead, and also similar children of any other denomination, Hebrew or Christian.

"I direct my executors hereinafter named, or such of them as shall qualify, to invest the funds arising from said estate in some safe, paying stocks as fast as they accumulate, and to hold the whole of the property and estate hereby devised and bequeathed for said school, and in their hands, until the proper steps have been taken by Congress, or the legislature of Virginia, or the said Hebrew Benevolent Congregations, to receive the same and discharge said executors."

The court, in its decision, extensively reviewed preceding cases, and held that, at common law, the trust would be void for want of a certain donee or beneficiary of the use or trust, whom the law could recognize. That it was uncertain which class of beneficiaries would be the parties in interest, and if the class were ascertainable, that the individuals thereof were indeterminate and unascertainable, and there was no ascertained beneficiary in whose favor performance might be enforced.

The court determined that the law of charitable trusts, as existing and enforced in England, being based on the statute of Elizabeth, was abrogated and annulled in the State by the act of 1788, which repealed the statute of Elizabeth; and that the legislature by that act intended to abrogate the entire system of indefinite trusts, which were understood at the time to be supported by that statute alone, as being opposed to the general policy of our government and to the spirit of our institutions.

The court also determined that the trustees named, viz., The People of the United States, or the State of Virginia, were incompetent to take as trustees, they being created for certain determinate political purposes, and having no other function or existence.* Nor could the Hebrew Congregations,

---

* The case of the Smithsonian Institute was adduced as an argument to show that the United States could take by devise. In that case Mr. Smithson, an Englishman by birth, and a citizen of that country, bequeathed to the United States all, or nearly all, of his property, to be

it was held, so act, as the trust was not within the acts or province of their incorporation; the one in New York could only take property for its own use, and the foreign corporations could not take and act as trustees of lands in this State. The court was further of opinion that the whole of the peculiar system of English jurisprudence, for supporting, regulating, and enforcing public or charitable uses, is not the law of the State of New York when in conflict with statutory prohibitions relative to uses and trusts.*

This case was afterwards followed by Bascom v. Albertson,† holding and approving the views of

applied to the establishment of an institution for the increase and diffusion of useful knowledge. But Wright, J., said that this furnished no evidence of capacity, simply as a political organization, to take and hold property for charitable purposes. That was an English charity, and the case was determined by the law of the domicile. It was a charity under the statute of Elizabeth, and administered as such, and took effect only on a law of Congress organizing the institution in the District of Columbia.

*In New York, as in many if not all the States, the law relating to trusts as it formerly existed in England in its intricate details, has been abolished, and only express, active trusts are permitted, where the trustee has some active duty to perform in the management of the estate. These express trusts are of four kinds: 1. To sell land for the benefit of creditors; 2. To sell, mortgage, or lease lands, to pay legacies or other charges; 3. Where the trustee is authorized to receive the rents and profits, and apply them to the use of some person during his life, or for a shorter period; 4. To receive rents and income to accumulate for the benefit of minors, to cease at majority. The same trusts only are allowed in California: Civil Code 857. It is therefore held that all trusts, for any purpose whatever, not coming under one of these four classes, are void, as it was apparent in the enumeration of these the legislature intended to exclude all others. Hence, in the drawing of wills, attention is most particularly needed to see that no trusts are created other than those above.

† 34 N. Y. 534. It is not uncommon for persons to devise property to the United States Government. The last case in New York was somewhat singular. It is in the case of United States v. Fox, in 52 N. Y. 530. The testator there devised " to the Government of the United

Levy v. Levy, which may now be considered as finally settling the law on this head in New York.

The statement of the law, as decided in New York, is not in harmony with the decisions in a large majority of the States. There is unquestionably a difference of opinion on this subject. The gist of inquiry is: Does the law of charitable uses exist in those States where the statute of Elizabeth is not in force, or has been repealed? Or, is the law appertaining to this subject founded on the common law, or is it the creation of the statute? There is no question that the weight of judicial opinion is greatly in favor of the doctrine that the law is not a creation of the statute, but is founded on the common law jurisdiction in the Court of Chancery, and as such can be administered by the courts in the absence of any special statute.*

The statute of Elizabeth is in force in Massachusetts, Pennsylvania, North Carolina, and Kentucky. It is not in force in Maryland, Virginia, California, and New York.

In some of the States, corporations are specially empowered by statute to take a certain amount of

States at Washington, District of Columbia, for the purpose of assisting to discharge the debt contracted by the war for the subjugation of the rebellious Confederate States." It was held that the government had no capacity to take. This case is now appealed to the Federal Courts, but with little prospect of reversal.

* Burbank v. Whitney, 24 Pick. 146; Beall v. Fox, 4 Ga. 404; Griffin v. Graham, 1 Hawks, 96; 7 Vt. 249; Vidal v. Gerard, 2 How. 127. The doctrine was elaborately argued and examined in the Gerard Will Case, 23 Penn. 54, and it was maintained that it was founded on the common law.

property by devise.* In New York, there is a statute, passed in 1860, which prohibits a person having a husband, wife, child, or parent, from devising or bequeathing to any charitable or literary corporation more than half of his or her estate, after payment of debts.

The most frequent and dangerous propensity which law has to check and guard against in testators is that of perpetuating in their family for generations vast property and estates. The desire of founding a family of vast wealth and influence to preserve one's property is not an uncommon one; it appeals to some of the dearest and most personal feelings of a man's nature; it is peculiarly gratifying to pride and pomp, and, if not limited and checked, would be dangerous to the public welfare, as it withdraws from the channels of trade and enterprise a large extent of property. Hence, every civilized country finds it necessary to define the extent of a man's control over his property, how long his volition can regulate its use after death, and to what purposes it shall be put. The common law permitted a control in this respect which would

---

* There are many institutions permitted by statute in New York to take property by devise or bequest. By Laws 1848, ch. 319, benevolent, charitable, literary, scientific, missionary, or Sabbath-school societies can take a devise or bequest, the clear annual income of which shall not exceed $10,000; but, to be valid, the will must be executed two months before testator's death. By Laws 1841, ch. 261, colleges and literary incorporated institutions are allowed to take for certain purposes. And, by Laws 1864, the State can take a devise for benefit and support of common schools. For these reasons, it is held the law of charitable uses is not so much required in New York; and, by special enactment, the legislature will incorporate societies to take a devise for pious, benevolent, or charitable purposes.

be entirely incompatible with our republican institutions and equality of our citizens.

Under that law, a man had the power to tie up his property and suspend the power of alienation, as it was termed, for any number of lives in being, and twenty-one years and a fraction afterwards. He could order the accumulation of the rents, income, or profits for a similar period. The case which first drew attention to the danger of such a power was one of the most famous in English law, and one that has since been a warning and an incentive to legislation both here and in England. Perhaps, for the amount involved, the tediousness and length of the litigation, and the singularity of the provisions, there has never been a more famous case than that of Thellusson v. Woodford,* tried before Lord Chancellor Loughborough, in the year 1798. The case afforded a remarkable instance of the unnatural meanness and ostentation of the testator, in depriving his immediate descendants of their just share of his fortune, not to found any noble charity, but that his fortune might accumulate in the hands of trustees, for the miserable satisfaction of enjoying in anticipation the wealth and aggrandizement of a distant posterity who should bear his name.

Peter Thellusson was born at Paris, of Swiss parentage, his father being a minister from Geneva to the French court. He settled in London as a merchant at an early age, was naturalized, and, on the foundation of a fortune of £10,000, raised the princely possessions which afterwards became the subject of litigation. It

* 4 Ves. 227.

is said that he was generally respected, and, though a severe economist, lived in a style suitable to his wealth. His three sons were all members of Parliament. In the sixty-first year of his age, being at the time in perfect health and legal sanity, he made and executed his last will, bearing date April 2d, 1796, and thereby disposed of his property upon trust during the natural lives of his three sons, and of the sons of each of these then in being, and of any such issue as any of his grandsons might have as should be living at the time of his decease. During the lives of the survivors or survivor of these persons mentioned, the trustees were to collect and receive the rents and invest them, and, upon the decease of the last survivor, all the accumulated estates should be divided into three lots, of equal value, and settled upon the eldest male lineal descendant then living of each of his three sons; and, if there should be a failure of male descendants of two of his said three sons, the sole male lineal descendant of the testator should become entitled to the whole three lots, consolidated into one huge mass of landed property. The property was thus tied up in the hands of trustees, and kept from enjoyment for three generations. Shortly after executing this extraordinary will, on 21st July, 1797, Mr. Thelusson died. The money which the will sought to accumulate was estimated at £600,000. An accountant of that time calculated the accumulation—limiting it to seventy-five years, the shortest possible period during which the property would be tied up—at £27,182,000, an immense sum, but which he deemed would be considerably less than the sum it would be likely to reach when the improvement of money at a higher rate and the lengthened duration of the last survivor were taken into account. It was estimated, by one of the counsel in the case, that if there were three descendants to take, each would have an income of £650,000 a year; if only one, he would have an income of £1,900,000 a year, more than double the revenue of the king's civil list, and surpassing the largest territorial fortune then known in Europe. Chancellor Kent, regarding it from his time, has said that if the limitation should extend to upwards of one hundred years, as it might, the property will amount to upwards of one hundred millions sterling.

The children brought an action to have the will set aside, but the court decided against them, and gave judgment confirming the trusts. The case attracted wide and deep attention from the magnitude of the fortune sought to be reared, and from the important principle of public policy involved. It was argued on both sides by the most eminent counsel at the bar, but nevertheless the Chancellor was compelled to hold the will valid, much, it is said, against his inclination. Next year, he was instrumental in getting Statute 39 and 40 Geo. III passed, restraining dispositions by way of accumulation to the life of the grantor, or twenty-one years after his decease, or the minority of any party living at the time of his decease.*

---

* In case the trust exceeds this term, it is void *in toto*, and not merely *pro tanto;* Griffiths v. Vere, 1 Ves. 136, 10 Penn. St. 326.

The property was accordingly left to accumulate; but the ambitious and vain visions of the testator and the alarm of the public were destined to disappointment. The structure which threatened even to overshadow the land in its ascending greatness has not risen to a disproportionate size. The operation of the trusts has proved practically a failure, as the accumulated mass of wealth is likely to fall far short of the amount which fanciful calculators had predicted. It has shared the inevitable fate of all such vast estates that get into the grist-mill of the lawyers. The litigation has been so expensive, that what with fees of lawyers, fees of courts, commissions to trustees, and the expense of management, the *corpus* of the estate has been pretty well eaten up. The expenses of management from January, 1816, to 1833, exceeded £122,700. The only increase in respect of income was £8,356, and an accumulation of capital of £326,364.

The extent of time to which property is allowed to accumulate is very carefully and strictly defined in our statutes. It is generally only during a person's minority, as in New York and California, and the same is believed to be the rule in general.*

The power of suspending the alienation of property by a devise is limited to lives in being in some States, or in others to *two* lives in being,† and no

---

* A direction to accumulate all the testator's estate for fifteen years by investment and reinvestment in bonds is valid in Illinois. Rhoads v. Rhoads, 43 Ill. 239.

But in New York an accumulation for three years, and also ten years, was held invalid : 4 Sandf. 442 ; 7 Barb. 590.

† In New York it is *two* lives ; in California, *any* lives in being : Civil Code, 715.

matter how short may be the duration, the suspension will be invalid if it is not made to depend on *life* as the condition of the limitation.* On this account, some very worthy and benevolent schemes of testators have failed.

The two lives must be designated. This may be done either by naming two persons in *particular*, or else by describing a *class* of persons, and bounding the suspense of alienation by the lives of the *two first* who shall die out of the class. The limitation may be restricted for a shorter period than two lives—it may be for a single life. The estate may also be limited so as to depend on some event besides life, provided it must vest within two lives; as an estate to A for ten years, if B and C, or either of them, shall so long live; here, the estate may determine either by the lapse of the ten years, or by the death of B and C; but it can in no event exceed two designated lives. So, an estate during minority, widowhood, or other stage of existence, through which *two* individuals may pass, would be good, because it could not by any possibility extend beyond two designated lives.†

---

* Schettler v. Smith, 41 N. Y. 328.

† The maximum period during which alienation may be suspended may, in one instance, under the New York statutes, and those of a great many other States, be suspended for two lives in being, and twenty-one years and a fraction afterwards, in certain cases of minority. For example, an estate to A for life, remainder to B for life, remainder to his children in fee, but in case such children shall die under the age of twenty-one years, then to D in fee. Here, it will be observed, the ownership may be legally suspended for the lives of A and B, and the actual infancy of B's children; but in no event can such suspension exceed that length of time before the remainder becomes vested. If one of the children reach twenty-one, D's remainder is cut off. In the example just given, suppose the children of B die before attaining twenty-one, and

These technical rules have rendered many a noble scheme abortive, and frustrated the benevolent and reformatory intentions of many a testator.

In the following instance, a testator's paternal solicitude for the reform of a wayward son, and his disapproval of his mode of life, were emphatically expressed; and an unfortunate oversight of this inflexible rule hindered the restraint the parent thought to place on his son after his decease. The father, however, with the usual confidence of a parent, had not abandoned all hope as to his ultimate recovery, for he thought fit to make him one of his executors, and thus placed him in the rather novel position of being a censor of his own conduct.

In the seventh clause of his will, after certain clear devises and bequests to other persons, was this recital and provision, viz: "Whereas, my son P, to whom sundry bequests are made in the following will, has unfortunately contracted habits of inebriation, and in consequence of which, I fear he would squander or misuse the bequests to him made, I do, therefore, annul and make void this will as to him, unless he reforms and continues a sober, industrious, and moral man, for the space of two years after my decease, giving to my executors satisfactory evidence

---

that B, at his death, leaves his wife *enceinte,* there would then be a suspension of alienation for a few months more than twenty-one years.

The extent to which variation from the ordinary term of gestation may take place in women, whether the birth be premature or protracted, is one of the difficult problems involved in medical jurisprudence. On this subject the highest medical authorities are at issue; some adhering closely to the regular period of forty weeks as the extreme term; while others extend their indulgence even to the utmost verge of eleven calendar months. See Long v. Blackall, 7 Term R. 104; Cadell v. Palmer, 1 Cl. & Finn. 372.

and assurance of a thorough reformation. And, therefore, it is my will, that the property so willed to him should be held in trust for him, not to exceed three years after my decease; and if within that time such reformation does not take place, I desire my said executors to divide his portion among such of my heirs as may seem to them most to need and deserve the same."*

It was held that this provision of the will was void, both as a *trust*, and as a *power in trust;* and that the son took the bequest notwithstanding.

The court deemed it "an unusual and extraordinary provision"; and as the period of suspension was measured by time alone, and not by *life*, this of itself rendered the provision nugatory.

It has been decided that if a bequest be made to certain trustees, to hold during the life of two persons designated, or until the legislature incorporate a hospital during the lifetime of the said persons, it is good.† It was in this way the will of Mr. Roosevelt was drawn, through which the Roosevelt Hospital in New York was founded. He bequeathed the residue of his estate, after other bequests, to nine trustees, five of whom were presidents of certain charitable institutions, for the establishment of an hospital for the reception and relief of sick and diseased persons, and directed them to apply to the legislature for a charter to incorporate the same, and in case the legislature should refuse to grant this within two years next

---

* Moore v. Moore, 47 Barb. 257.
† Burrill v. Boardman, 43 N. Y. 254.

after his death, *provided two lives named in his will should continue so long*, then the trustees were to pay over the same to the United States for a similar purpose.

It was held that this provision did not violate the statute of perpetuities, but that the corporation could take only in case the charter was granted within the two lives named. There was no need to consider the validity of the devise to the United States. The charter was granted in February, 1864, and now the hospital stands conspicuous among the charities of New York city.

An oversight in the observance of this rule against perpetuities caused the failure of a grand and meritorious scheme conceived by the late Mr. Rose of New York. He died in 1860, and left a large amount of property—estimated at two millions of dollars—to found an institution called the "Rose Beneficent Association,"* whose object it was to educate and train waifs picked up on the streets, and make them useful citizens. He gave the bequests upon the contingency of raising $300,000 from other sources within *five years*. If that sum was not so raised, the estate was given to other charitable beneficiaries. The utmost limit of the suspension was five years, but it was not circumscribed by lives as the Statute of Perpetuities requires, and it was adjudged to be void. It should be stated as a warning that this will of Mr. Rose was drawn by himself.

---

* Rose v. Rose, 4 Abb. Ct. App., Dec., 198.

The case occupied a long time in litigation, and the subject of charitable bequests was most exhaustively examined.*

* The argument of Prof. Dwight, one of the counsel, in two volumes, presents a marvelous and most scholarly amount of research upon the law of charitable uses, from the earliest times.

CHAPTER VI.

Revocation of Wills.

It is one of the well-understood qualities of a will, at the present time, that it is revocable during the testator's lifetime. It was shown, in a former part of this work, that this quality did not in early times attach to a will; that a will, at first, was in the nature of an executed contract; a conveyance, in fact, and irrevocable.* However, as a will has no effect until death, it necessarily follows that a person has full control of the subject-matter, and can change his mind as he pleases regarding its disposition so long as he lives. This is now accepted as a postulate in the law of wills.† The only inquiry, therefore, will be as to what acts or occurrences shall be deemed sufficient to revoke a will previously made.

There are two modes in which a will may be revoked: *First*, it may be revoked by the happening of some events subsequent to the making as, in the judgment of law, will amount to a revocation. We

---

* See page 31.

† Swinburne, Part 7, Sec. 14, says: "Concerning the making of a latter testament, so large and ample is the liberty of making testaments that a man may, as oft as he will, make a new testament, even until his last breath; neither is there any cautel under the sun to prevent this liberty; but no man can die with two testaments, and therefore the last and newest is of force; so that, if there were a thousand testaments, the last of all is the best of all, and makes void the former."

may term this an implied revocation. *Secondly*, it may be revoked by a certain deliberate act of the maker, intending to cancel a previous will, or with *animo revocandi*, as the legal phrase is.

The events which would operate to produce an implied revocation of a will were formerly a subject of wide and constant discussion. The courts in England, and until lately in this country, occupied themselves very frequently in discussing this subject of implied revocation, and, for a long time, there was no general agreement on the precise events that would, in the judgment of law, amount to a revocation. At an early period in the English law, it was determined that the marriage of a *feme sole* was sufficient to revoke a will made by her previous to her marriage. It was expressed thus, in the quaint language of the time: "It was adjudged, on great deliberation, that the taking of a husband, and the coverture at the time of her death, was a countermand of the will."[*] This enunciation of the law has ever since prevailed as a principle in the law of wills. But a similar marriage in the case of a man did not have the same effect. The courts were at first not agreed as to whether the birth of a child after the making of a will would be sufficient to effect a revocation. In one case, it was decided that this event alone did not amount to a revocation;[†] but in another case, where there were *four* children born subsequently to the making of the will, this, combined with other circumstances, was held to be a revocation.[‡] It came to pass that the

---

[*] 4 Co. Rep. 60.   [†] Doe v. Barford, 4 Man. & S. 16.
[‡] Johnston v. Johnston, 1 Phillim. 447.

courts became finally agreed on the question that marriage, together with the birth of issue, was sufficient to effect a revocation of a will.*

In the application of this rule, cases of great hardship have sometimes occurred; but it has been steadily adhered to, even under circumstances in regard to real estate, at least; as where the testator left his wife *enceinte* without knowing it, as was the case in Doe v. Barford, above, where Lord Ellenborough held that the birth of a child *alone*, even under these circumstances, was not sufficient to revoke the will which was made after marriage. He said: "Marriage, indeed, and the having of children, where *both* these circumstances have occurred, has been deemed a presumptive revocation; but it has not been shown that either of them *singly* is sufficient. I remember a case some years ago of a sailor who made his will in favor of a woman with whom he cohabited, and afterwards went to the West Indies, and married a woman of considerable substance; and it was held, notwithstanding the hardship of the case, that the will swept away from the widow every shilling of the property, for the birth of a child must necessarily concur to constitute an implied revocation. In Doe v. Lancashire, 5 T. R. 49, it was adjudged that marriage and the pregnancy of the wife, with the knowledge of the husband, and the subsequent birth of a posthumous child, came within the rule, the same as if the child had been born during the parent's life."

This subject was elaborately examined by Chan-

---

* Wellington v. Wellington, 4 Burr. 2165.

cellor Kent, in the case of Brush v. Wilkins,* where the authorities from the earliest times were quoted and examined, and the same conclusion reached.

This inquiry is not of much practical importance now, either here or in England, for statutory enactments have laid down the law precisely and satisfactorily as to what circumstances shall be deemed sufficient to produce the revocation of a will. And this is very desirable, since much uncertainty and discussion is thereby avoided, and the devolution of property exactly determined.† There is scarcely a State we know of where statutes have not been passed, setting the matter at rest, and fixing the law on the subject.

By the recent English statute, wills are held absolutely revoked by the subsequent marriage of the testator, whether made by a man or woman, unless such will be made in execution of certain powers; and it is further provided that no will shall be revoked, by any presumption of intention, on the ground of an alteration of circumstances.

In the statutes of the different States there is this difference: In some, the birth of a child after making a will, where such child is unprovided for, will work a revocation; while in others, it will only

---

* 4 Johns. Ch. 506. Of course, this rule was only good where the issue of the marriage were otherwise unprovided for, or had no means of maintenance.

† The law respecting implied revocations was a fruitful source of difficult and expensive litigation, and often defeated the intention of testators, instead of carrying it into effect. Lord Mansfield has said that some of the decisions on this head had brought " a scandal on the law"; and, on another occasion, he remarked " that all revocations not agreeable to the intention of the testator are founded on artificial and absurd reasoning." 3 Burr. 491.

revoke it *pro tanto*, that is, so as to allow the child to have the same share as if the parent died intestate.

In Ohio, Indiana, Illinois, and Connecticut, the birth of a child avoids the will *in toto*.*

By the statute laws of Maine, Vermont, New Hampshire, Massachusetts, New York, New Jersey, Pennsylvania, Delaware, and California, children born after the making of the will inherit as if the parent died intestate, unless the will comprises some provision for them, or they are particularly referred to in it. The will is thus revoked *pro tanto*.†

In Virginia and Kentucky, the birth of a child after the will, if there were none previously, revokes the will, unless the child dies unmarried or an infant.‡

The statute law of some States goes further, and entitles not only children but their *issue* to claim portion of testator's estate, if such children were unprovided for, and unmentioned in the will. This is the case in the California code,§ and in Maine, New Hampshire,|| Rhode Island, and Massachusetts.

By the New York revised statutes, if a will disposes of the whole estate, marriage and the birth of a child revoke the will, if either the wife or child survive the testator.¶ Parol evidence is not admissible to rebut this presumption. Wherever the question has arisen, it has generally been held,

---

* Ash v. Ash, 9 Ohio, 383; Stat. Ohio, (1831) p. 243; Stat. Ind. 1821; Stat. Ill. 1829; G. Laws, Conn. p. 370, last edition.
† 4 Kent, 525; Cal. Civ. Code, 1306.
‡ 4 Kent, 526.
§ Sec. 1307.
|| Gage v. Gage, 9 Foster, 533.
¶ 2 Rev. Stat. 64.

even in the States where by statute children omitted in the will of the parent are entitled to the same share of his estate as if he had died intestate, that marriage and the birth of issue, after the making of a will, do amount to an implied revocation of the will.*

In many of the States, marriage alone, after making the will, amounts to a revocation. In Virginia, it is revoked by marriage;† also, in West Virginia; so in California, unless a provision be made for the wife.‡ In others, it only revokes the will *pro tanto*, as in Pennsylvania and Delaware.§ In the State of Illinois, where the husband and wife are made heirs to each other, marriage by the testator after making his will, wherein no provision in contemplation of such new relation exists, amounts to a revocation.‖ The marriage of a woman after making her will, will produce a revocation in general. It is so in New York and California;¶ and in California it is not revived by death of the husband. This provision is in harmony with the early cases in England.**

It must not be inferred from the previous statement that a testator has no power to disinherit or cut off a child. The law does not withhold this power; it only presumes, by the omission to men-

---

* Redfield, I, 293.
† Rev. Stat. 1849, Ch. 122
‡ Civil Code, 1290. So in Rhode Island, Rev. Stat. Ch. 154.
§ Tomlinson v. Tomlinson, 1 Ashm. 224.
‖ Tyler v. Tyler, 19 Ill. 151.
¶ 2 N. Y. Rev. Stat. 64; Civil Code, 1299.
** Cotter v. Layer, 2 P. Wms. 623.

tion the name of a child in a will, that the claim of that child was overlooked by the testator, and the court, exercising its equitable power, interferes on behalf of such child to see it gets its due share of the property. But where the intention is expressed, and much more so where a reason is given, for cutting off a child from a participation in a testator's property, the courts cannot interfere in behalf of such disinherited child, unless on some imputation of insanity or undue influence.

Another, and a more usual mode in which a will may be revoked, is by an express deliberate act of the testator. This may be done by a subsequent testamentary document, or by some physical destruction or cancelation of the will. A very common phrase used in a will is: "And I hereby revoke all former and other wills and testamentary dispositions by me at any time heretofore made." However, the insertion of a clause like this is not of much importance, as a will professing to dispose of the *whole* of a testator's property necessarily displaces and supersedes all antecedent testamentary instruments.* Such a clause might be useful in those instances in which the intention to dispose of the entire estate was not so clearly manifested as to preclude attempts to adopt, wholly or partially, the contents of former wills as part of the testator's disposition; since a will may be composed of *several* papers of *different* dates, each

---

* In re Fisher, 4 Wis. 254; Simmons v. Simmons, 26 Barb. 68; Smith v. McChesney, 15 N. J. Ch. 359.

professing to be such when they are capable of standing together.*

Mere proof of the execution of a subsequent will, therefore, is not sufficient to invalidate a prior will. There must be proof of a clause of revocation, or there must be plainly contrary or inconsistent provisions.† And where the contents of the last will cannot be ascertained, it is not a revocation of the former will. This was decided by the Court of King's Bench in England, more than one hundred and fifty years ago, in the case of Hutchins v. Bassett;‡ and that decision was subsequently affirmed upon a writ of error in the House of Lords. In the subsequent case of Harwood v. Goodright,§ which came before the Court of King's Bench in 1774, it was held that a former will was not revoked by a subsequent one, the contents of which could not be ascertained; although it was found by a special verdict that the disposition which the testator made of his property by the last will was different from that made by the first will, but in what particulars the jurors could not ascertain. This case also was carried to the House of Lords upon a writ of error, and the judgment was affirmed. As these two decisions of the court of *dernier resort* in England were previous to the Revolution, they conclusively settle the law on this subject here.‖

* Campbell v. Logan, 2 Bradf. 90.
† Cutto v. Gilbert, 9 Moore, P. C. C. 131.
‡ Mod. 203.
§ 1 Cowp. 87.
‖ Nelson v. McGiffert, 3 Barb. Ch. 162. In some States this is settled by statute. Thus, in California, an antecedent will is not revived by the

Again, where there are several codicils or other testamentary papers of different dates, it is a question of intention upon all the circumstances of the case, which and how far either is a revocation of another, or whether the dispositions of the latter are to be considered as additional and cumulative to those of the prior. Parol evidence, however, is not to be admitted in order to investigate the *animus* with which the act was done, unless there is such doubt and ambiguity, *on the face of the papers*, as requires the aid of extrinsic evidence to explain it.*

In a late case,† the subject of receiving parol evidence in regard to the fact and intent of the revocation of wills, is very carefully examined, and the principle declared, that where the testator executed a will, and subsequently executed another, which he took away with him, and which on his decease could not be found, the earlier one being found, that the solicitor who drew the will, or any other witness familiar with its contents, might give evidence thereof; and it appearing that the provisions of the later one were inconsistent with those of the former, it was held to amount to a revocation. The practice, in the American courts, of receiving parol evidence of the contents of a lost will, seems to be universal, and without question, notwithstand-

---

revocation of a subsequent will unless an intention appear: Civil Code, 1297. The same in New York: 2 Rev. Stat. 66.

* Wms. Exrs. 136 and cases cited. The general effect of a subsequent will in revoking one of an earlier date, by reason of its inconsistent provisions, is very extensively discussed in the late and important case of Colvin v. Warford, 20 Md. 357.

† Brown v. Brown, 8 El. & Bl. 876.

ing the stringent statutory requirements in regard to the mode of executing wills.* The evidence must come from witnesses who have read the will, and whose recollection of its contents is trustworthy.† But in cases of fraud, more indulgence is allowed to the proof, and in Jones v. Murphy,‡ the court said: "It is better, surely, that a person should die intestate than that the spoliator should be rewarded for his villainy." The English courts do not grant the same indulgence to admit alleged lost wills to probate. In a late case, where the contents of the will were propounded for probate after a delay of seven years, and no sufficient explanation given of the manner or cause of the loss, and when no draft of the will could be produced, but only oral proof of its contents, due execution, and that it could not have been revoked, probate was denied.§

The question as to what extent a codicil shall control the provisions in the will is not always easy of solution. Each case depends almost exclusively upon its own peculiar circumstances, and will not, therefore, be much guide to others, unless the facts are very similar. But the general rule of construction is that already stated, to allow all the provi-

---

* Howard v. Davis, 2 Binney, 406; Jackson v. Betts, 6 Cow. 483; Steele v. Price, 5 B. Mon. 58; 8 Met. 486.
† 7 B. Mon. 408.
‡ 8 Watts & Serg. 275.
§ Wharram v. Wharram, 10 Jur. N. S. 499. A will and codicil were torn to pieces by a testator's eldest son, after the death of his father; the pieces were saved, by which, and by oral evidence, the court arrived at the substance of those instruments, and in effect pronounced for them. Foster v. Foster, 1 Addams, 462.

sions of the will to stand which are not inconsistent with those of the codicil, and in determining this, to seek for the intention of the testator, as far as practicable.* Where a codicil refers to the former of two inconsistent wills, by date, as the last will of the testator, it has the effect to cancel the intermediate will, and evidence of mistake cannot be admitted.† Where a codicil named the wife as " sole executrix of this my will," it was held that the appointment of other executors in the will was revoked.‡

It has been held that a revocation is not valid, in most of the American States, unless done with the same formality required in the execution of the will itself.§

Thus, writing the word "obsolete" on the margin of his will by the testator, but without signing the same in any of the modes allowed by law, will not amount to a revocation.‖

In a somewhat recent case in Pennsylvania, the question of revocation arose, in regard to a bequest to charity.¶ The court held that, where there are two wills, in some respects inconsistent, the latter revokes the former only so far as they are inconsistent with each other, unless there is an express clause of revocation. But where the property given specifically in the first will is, in the second, contained in a general devise to the same objects, and

---

* Patch v. Graves, 3 Denio, 348 ; 28 Vt. 274.
† 4 Ves. 610.
‡ 3 Sw. & Tr. 478.
§ 14 Mass. 208; Hine v. Hine, 31 Penn. 246.
‖ Lewis v. Lewis, 2 W. & S. 455.
¶ Price v. Maxwell, 28 Penn. 23.

for the same purpose, and the appointment of other executors, there is a manifest inconsistency, and it evinces an intention that both wills should not stand.

Many times it happens that a testator, dissatisfied with an executor or devisee named in his will, erases the name of such executor or devisee; but this will not always effect his purpose, as it should be done by a subsequent codicil, properly executed. Thus, where a testator (without a republication of his will) made alterations and corrections in it, with the intent, not to destroy it, but to enlarge and extend a devise already made, it was held not a revocation of the devise.*

The physical destruction or cancelation of a will by a testator is the most palpable and unmistakable mode of its revocation. In what manner or in what different modes this may be done was first laid down in the Statute of Frauds, where revocation was to be effected by "burning, canceling, tearing, or obliterating" the will. These four phrases have been generally adopted and inserted in our statutes, with either some modification or enlargement.

The enumeration of these several modes for the destruction of a will by a testator, to amount to its revocation, has not prevented controversy and un-

---

* Howard v. Halliday, 7 Johns. R. 394. If two wills, in duplicate, were in possession of the testator, and he destroyed one, did this, in effect, work a revocation? This was in some doubt. The California Code has set at rest this question for that State, in Sec. 1295, where it is provided that a destruction of one of the copies shall amount to a revocation. See Onions v. Tyrer, 2 Vern. 742.

certainty; for law cannot define acts in words so precisely and unmistakably as to preclude all doubt and quibbling. There are sure to be some who will play upon words—a mental recreation to which legal minds are somewhat given—and who will insist upon an exact literal conformity when a revocation is sought to be maintained under this provision. It would seem to an ordinary mind hardly possible to admit of a doubt that *cutting* a will was, in effect, equivalent to *tearing;* yet a legal quibble went so far as to question this, when it became necessary to decide that cutting was, in effect, the same as tearing.* Probably, the legislature of West Virginia took into consideration a knotty question of this kind, and took good care to save a legal luminary stumbling over a question of this sort; for, by the statute of that State, it is provided that a revocation in this manner may be effected by "*cutting*, tearing, burning, obliterating, canceling, or destroying the same."

To avoid any limited construction of the words as used in the English Statute of Frauds, it is generally provided in our statutes that a revocation may be made as in that statute, or by *otherwise destroying* the will.† This cuts off a great deal of uncertain construction, and removes a great tempta-

---

* Hobbs v. Knight, 1 Curteis, 289. And the cutting out of the principal part, as the signature of the testator, or of the witnesses, will be a revocation of the whole will: 1 Jarman, 161.

† Where the word "destroying" is used in the statute, as one mode of revocation, it is generally held to include all modes of defacing not specifically enumerated in the statute, and does not require an absolute and entire destruction. Johnson v. Brailsford, 2 Nott & McCord, 272.

tion for fine legal distinctions. In the New York statute, a revocation is effected in this way, if the will is *burnt, torn, obliterated, canceled, or destroyed*, with intent and for the purpose of revoking the same.*

The statute very wisely requires two things to be combined before it concludes that a will is revoked. There must be the *act* of destruction with the *intent*, or the *animo revocandi*, as the law terms it. Under the English statute, it had been determined that the mere acts named will not constitute a valid revocation unless done with the intent to revoke.† Lord Mansfield here explains very graphically the acts which might often occur, which would destroy the writing, but would not amount to a revocation of the will; as, if a man were to throw ink upon his will instead of sand; or, having two wills, of different dates, should direct the former to be destroyed, and by mistake the latter is canceled. In neither case would it amount to a revocation of the will, although the writing were irrevocably gone.

Revocation is an act of the mind which must be demonstrated by some outward and visible sign. The statute prescribes what those signs are. If any of these are performed in the slightest manner, joined with a declared intent to revoke, it will be an effectual revocation.‡

It would be manifestly a harsh and an unjust

---

* 2 Rev. Stat. 66. It is the same in California: Civil Code, 1292.
† Burtenshaw v. Gilbert, 1 Cowp. 49.
‡ Dan v. Brown, 4 Cow. 490.

construction to place upon the statute, that because a will was destroyed in any one of the modes pointed out, that a strict interpretation required a revocation. Hence, where the destruction was done unadvisedly, or by some other casualty, it was held, it could not amount to a revocation. Thus, where a will was gnawed to pieces by rats, but the pieces, being collected, were afterwards put together, the will was admitted to probate.*

And in Perkes v. Perkes,† a testator having quarreled with a person who was a devisee in his will, in a fit of passion took the will out of the desk, and, addressing some words to a bystander, tore it twice through, but was prevented from proceeding further by the interference of the other person and the submission of the devisee; and he then became calm, put up the pieces and said: "It is a good job it is no worse"; and after fitting the pieces together, added: "There is nothing ripped that will be any signification to it." The jury found that the act of canceling was incomplete at the time the testator was stopped; and the court was of opinion that that conclusion was right, and that the will was not revoked.

Where a testator, with an intent to revoke his will, endeavors to destroy it in some of the modes pointed out, but through the fraud, imposition, or other deception of a person, the act is prevented being completed, it shall not prevent a revocation. The following case is a striking one, and illustrates

---

* Etheringham v. Etheringham, Alcyn, 2.   † 3 B. & Ald. 489.

this principle. A testator, (who had for two months declared himself discontented with his will) being one day in bed near the fire, ordered M W, who attended him, to fetch his will, which she did and delivered it to him, it being then whole, only somewhat erased. He opened it, looked at it, then gave it something of a rip with his hands, and so tore it as almost to tear a bit off, then rumpled it together, and threw it upon the fire, but it fell off. It must soon have been burnt, had not M W taken it up, which she did, and put it in her pocket. The testator did not see her take it up, but seemed to have some suspicion of it, as he asked her what she was about, to which she made little or no answer. The testator, several times afterwards, said that was not and should not be his will, and bid her destroy it. She said at first, "so I will, when you have made another"; but afterwards, upon his repeated inquiries, she told him that she had destroyed it, though in fact it was never destroyed, that she believed he imagined it was destroyed. She asked him who his estate would go to when the will was burnt; he answered, to his sister and her children. He afterwards told a person that he had destroyed his will, and should make no other until he had seen his brother, J M, and desired the person to tell his brother that he wanted to see him. He afterwards wrote to his brother, saying, "I have destroyed my will, which I made, for upon serious consideration, I was not easy in my mind about that will," and desired him to come down, saying, "If I die intestate, it will cause uneasiness." The testator, however, died without making another will. The jury, with the concurrence of the judge, thought this a sufficient revocation of the will, and on a motion for a new trial it was so held, and that throwing it on the fire, with an intent to burn, though it was only very slightly singed and fell off, was sufficient within the statute.*

The English courts are more strict in requiring a substantial compliance with the statute than our courts are. In the American cases, the intention is looked upon as the most material and controlling element: as where a testator asked for his will on his sick bed, and was handed an old letter, which he destroyed, supposing it to be his will, it was held to be a good revocation.†

And where a testator threw his will upon the fire, *animo revocandi*, and it was taken off and preserved, before any words were burned, and without the testator's knowledge, it was decided, by a very able court, that it did amount to revocation.‡ So, where a testatrix burns a paper, which she supposes to be her will, and by mistake or the fraud of others burns a different paper, and remains under this misapprehension during her life, it amounts, in law, to a revocation.§ But in a case in Vermont it was held that the mere intention or desire to revoke one's will, until carried into effect in the manner

---

* Bibb v. Thomas, 2 W. Bl. 1043.
† Pryor v. Coggin, 17 Ga. 444.
‡ White v. Carter, 1 Jones (N. C.) Law, 197.
§ Smiley v. Gambill, 2 Head, 164.

prescribed in the statute, can have no effect; however, if such intention is defeated by fraud, a court of equity will prevent a party moving from any benefit of such fraud.*

The two words "canceling" and "obliterating" have occasioned more uncertainty than the others used in the statute, because it is not so easily or exactly determined what acts shall amount to a cancelation and what to an obliteration of the will. In one case, the will was found with another testamentary paper, but the place in which the names of the attesting witnesses should have appeared, upon the latter, was scratched over with a pen and ink, so that no letter of a name could be deciphered: it was held that this paper was thereby revoked, and the will was admitted to probate alone.†

It seems to be settled, that from the fact of interlineations and erasures appearing upon the face of a will, no such presumption arises, as in the case of deeds and other instruments, that they were made before execution. But in regard to a will the case is different. Hence, where the testator makes an alteration in his will by erasure and interlineation, or in any other mode, without authenticating such alteration by a new attestation in the presence of witnesses, or other form required by the statute, the will, therefore, stands in legal force the same as it did before, so far as it is legible after the attempted alteration,‡ but if the former reading cannot be

---

*Blanchard v. Blanchard, 32 Vt. 62.   †7 Jur. N. S. 52.
‡1 Jarman, 133.

made out by inspection of the paper, probate is decreed, and such illegible portions are treated as blanks.

In a case in Pennsylvania,* where the will was found in the testator's private desk, with the seals of the envelope broken, and a black line drawn through the name of the testator, and there was no evidence how or with what intent it was done, it was held a sufficient revocation. Vice-Chancellor Wood, in a case in New York,† decided that where a testator, having torn off the signature from the first four sheets of his will, and struck his pen through the signature upon the remaining sheet, the *animus revocandi* being proved, it was a sufficient revocation.

The clearest statement of the law on this head was made by an eminent judge, whose language very clearly sums up the law. Chief Justice Ruffin, in a case in North Carolina,‡ says:

"The statute does not define what is such a cancelation or obliteration as shall amount, conclusively, to a revocation of a will. Burning, or the utter destruction of the instrument by any other means, are clear indications of purpose which cannot be mistaken.

"But obliterating may be accidental, or may be partial, and therefore is an equivocal act, in reference to the whole instrument, and particularly to the parts that are unobliterated. So, canceling, by

---

* Bap. Church v. Roberts, 2 Penn. 110.
† 1 Johns. Ch. 530.
‡ Bethell v. Moore, 2 Dev. & Batt. 311.

merely drawing lines through the signature, leaving it legible, and leaving the body of the instrument entire, is yet more equivocal, especially if the instrument be preserved by the party, and placed in his depository as a valuable paper. It may be admitted that the slightest act of cancelation, with intent to revoke absolutely, although such intent continue but for an instant, is a total and perpetual revocation; and the paper can only be set up as a new will. But that is founded upon the intent. Without such intention, no such effect can follow; for the purpose of the mind gives the character to the act. When, therefore, there appears a cancelation, it becomes necessary to look at the extent of it, at all the conduct of the testator, at what he proposed doing at the time, at what he did afterwards. . . . . . For, although every act of canceling imports, *prima facie*, that it is done *animo revocandi*, yet it is but a presumption which may be repelled by accompanying circumstances."

There seems to be no question, according to Jarman,* that, under the Statute of Frauds and other similar statutes, as *parts* of an entire will may be revoked, in the same mode the whole may be so revoked. The same rule has been adopted in this country, to some extent. The question was ably examined by Surrogate Bradford, in a case in New York.† In that case, a testator, after his will had been prepared and executed, becoming dissatisfied with one of the devisees, his own daughter, struck

---

* 1 Jarman, 125.   † McPherson v. Clark, 3 Bradf. 92.

out the devise to her, which was contained in these words: "To my beloved and only daughter, Sarah Ann McPherson, I give and bequeath," etc. In a note to the foot of the page, he gave as a reason for striking out this devise, the bad treatment of his daughter, and afterwards altered a phrase in his will where "children" was used, and substituted "sons" instead, so as to exclude the said daughter. In examining this question, the learned Surrogate assumed that a *part* of a will might be obliterated in the same mode as the whole, and referred to various decisions in support of this view. He, however, held that, as the subsequent alteration, substituting "sons" for "children," was invalid, not having been re-witnessed, as is required, that the obliteration of the devise was not effectual as to that part, and could not be treated as a revocation.

In Kentucky, in the case of Brown's Will,* it was declared that a cancelation of a portion of the devises, the testator's signature being left untouched, did not affect the residue of the dispositions, which remained unaltered, the testator's intention not to revoke them being clearly established.

* 1 B. Mon. 57.

CHAPTER VII.

WILLS AS AFFECTED BY DOMICILE.

There is a certain respect paid by the laws of one nation or community to those of another, which is termed international comity, which, for general convenience and utility, is observed and regarded by tribunals when certain acts done in one place are to be construed in another.

Of course, such comity is merely conventional—there is no binding obligation to enforce it; but from long observance, and the customary regard tribunals have given to certain rules of international comity, these rules have been so long sanctioned by precedent and authority as now to have the force of law. The law relating to wills as affected by domicile is, to a great extent, founded on such rules of international comity, or *leges gentium*.

The principles of law appertaining to this subject are well settled and recognized, and are now invariably acted upon. The language of wills is supposed to speak the sense of the testator according to the received laws or usages of the country where he is domiciled, by a sort of tacit reference to them, unless there is something in the language which repels or controls such a conclusion.

In regard to personalty, (in an especial manner) the law of the place of the testator's domicile governs in the distribution thereof, and will govern in the interpretation of wills, unless it is manifest the testator had the laws of some other country in his own view. This is usually expressed by the legal formula, that, with regard to personal property, the *lex domicilii* governs.* The law on this subject has never been more clearly expressed, or better summarized, than by the Lord Chancellor, in the case of Enohin v. Wylie.† His lordship there says: "I hold it to be now put beyond the possibility of a question, that the administration of the personal estate of a deceased person belongs to the court of the country where the deceased was domiciled at his death. All questions of testacy or intestacy belong to the judge of the domicile. It is the right and duty of that judge to constitute the personal representative of the deceased. To the courts of the domicile belong the interpretation and construction of the will of the testator. To determine who are the next of kin, or heirs of the personal estate of the testator, is the prerogative of the judge of the domicile. In short, the court of the domicile is the *forum concursus* to which the legatees under the will of a testator,‡ or the parties entitled to the distribution of the estate of an intestate, are required to resort."

As a will is governed in its interpretation according to the law of the place where the testator had his domicile, therefore, if a testator, born and domi-

---

* 2 Doug. (Mich.) 515.

† 8 Jur. N. S. 897.

‡ Legatees are entitled to be paid in the money of the country in which the testator is domiciled and the will is made. 2 Atk. 465 ; 2 Bro. C. C. 39.

ciled in England during his whole life, should, by his will, give his personal estate to his heir-at-law, that the *descriptio personæ* would have reference to, and be governed by, the import of the terms in the sense of the laws of England.* The import of them might be very different if the testator were born or domiciled in France, Pennsylvania, or Massachusetts.

To ascertain what the testator means, we must first ascertain *what was his domicile*, and whether he had reference to the laws of that place or the laws of any foreign country.†

The law of the domicile governs as to the proper mode of execution and attestation of wills of personal property; hence it is accepted as a rule of

---

* Harrison v. Nixon, 9 Peters, 483.

† To determine a person's domicile is sometimes a matter of some difficulty. It is determined on two principles: the *fact* of one's residence, and the *intent* of remaining there as at one's home; or it depends upon *habitation* and the *animo manendi*. Residence and domicile are not convertible terms, because they are not the same things. The Roman definition has been admired for its expressiveness and force. It is there defined: "It is not doubted that individuals have a home in that place where each one has established his hearth, and the sum of his possessions and fortunes; whence he will not depart if nothing calls him away; whence if he has departed he seems to be a wanderer, and if he returns he ceases to wander." (Code, lib. 10, tit. 39.) It must be assumed as a fact that every person has a domicile, or home, and the domicile of origin remains until another is obtained, not by merely moving or changing, but by leaving it with no intention of returning, without *animo revertendi*. But an intention to change is not sufficient to alter a domicile until it is actually changed. Therefore, death *en route* does not alter domicile. (State v. Hallet, 8 Ala. 159.) One who goes abroad, *animo revertendi*, does not change his domicile, because only the fact of residence is changed, and not the intent. But if he remains very long abroad, and in one place, the intent may be inferred from the fact. The Supreme Court of the United States have intimated that an exercise of the right of suffrage would be the highest evidence, and almost conclusive against the party. (Shelton v. Tiffin, 6 How. 185.)

universal application, that a will of personal property, duly admitted to probate where a person has his domicile, is conclusive on all other courts, and is sufficient to pass personal property, wherever situated.*

It has been a subject of discussion, whether a will, made by a person according to the law of his domicile at the time when made, will be operative if he subsequently changes his domicile, and dies in his new domicile. This is a question of grave importance, and one on which there is a serious conflict of authority. The question is then presented, as to what law should govern, whether the law of the domicile *at the time the will was made*, or the law of the domicile *at the time of decease.*

This question arose in New York, in a case which passed through all the subordinate courts, and was finally determined by its highest court, after very thorough and learned examination. It was the case of Moultrie v. Hunt.†

The testator, Benjamin F. Hunt, resided at Charleston, and there made his will, in August, 1849, conformable to the laws of South Carolina. He subsequently removed to New York, where he

---

* The doctrine was well settled in a very early case in Pennsylvania, decided by Judge Tilgham, in 1808 : the case of Desasbats v. Berquier, 1 Binn. 336 ; and this case has ever since been quoted and approved as a good statement of the law on this point. There, a will was executed in St. Domingo by a person domiciled there, and sought to be enforced in Pennsylvania, where the effects of the deceased were. It appeared not to have been executed according to the laws of St. Domingo, though it was conceded that it would have been a good will if executed by a citizen of Pennsylvania. The alleged will was held to be invalid.

† 23 N. Y. 394.

established his domicile, and where he died. His will was attested, at his request, by three witnesses; but Mr. Hunt did not state to the witnesses the nature of the paper which he requested them to attest, and, therefore, omitted to comply with one of the requisites of the statute in New York, which requires a publication of the will, to be a valid execution thereof.

The Surrogate, when the case came before him, decided to admit the will to probate, and made a decree accordingly. This decree was affirmed by the Supreme Court, whence it was taken on appeal to the Court of Appeals, and it was there reversed, a very able judge (Denio) writing the opinion of the court. His opinion was very able and elaborate, and a thorough examination was made of all the authorities. He holds that a will cannot operate so as to confer rights of property until the death of the testator, until which event it is, in its essence, ambulatory and revocable. Therefore, it is the law in force *at the death of the testator* that should govern as to the due execution of a will and the capacity of a testator. He illustrated this in the case of the legislature making laws that would have the effect of invalidating wills already made, and shows that where a will was witnessed by but two witnesses, three being required at the time it was made, that it was subsequently validated by a law in force at the decease of the testator, allowing two witnesses to attest a will. He quotes from Story* to show that it is the law of the domicile *at*

---

*Confl. Laws, Sec. 481; Adams v. Wilbur, 2 Sumner, 266.

the time of death that should govern as to the proper execution, and he approves that doctrine, and holds it applicable to this case; which, it was held, should be governed by the law of New York, the law of the domicile of the testator at the time of his death, and therefore Mr. Hunt was considered as dying intestate in respect to personal property in New York. Judge Redfield, in his work on wills, approves of this doctrine,* and the same point has been decided in Missouri.†

The question, however, is not free from doubt, as very able jurists differ on it. As far as New York is concerned, it has settled the law there.

The case of the will of General Kosciusko, before the Supreme Court of the United States, in December, 1852, was in many respects the most notable and interesting case on this subject ever examined. In that case, it was necessary to examine, carefully and strictly, the law of wills as affected by domicile, and the manner of acquiring a domicile, and the mode of proving it. This case, besides its importance in a legal point of view, is of much public interest, as bringing up some memorable incidents connected with our revolutionary struggle and the eminent personages who participated in that struggle. It is found in the case of Ennis v. Smith,‡ and we will be justified in stating the facts somewhat in detail.

Kosciusko made four wills, one in the United States in 1798, another in Paris in 1806, the third

---

* Wills, I, 404.   † Nat v. Coons, 10 Mo. 543.   ‡ 14 How. 400.

and fourth in Switzerland, whilst sojourning there during the years 1816 and 1817. In his third will there was a revocation clause, canceling the first and second wills, in these words:

"Je revoque tous les testaments et codiciles que J'ai pu faire avant le présent auquel seul Je m'arrête comme contenant mes dernierès volantes."

The object of the suit in the Supreme Court was as to the disposition of a fund belonging to Kosciusko in the United States, which, it was claimed, was undisposed of by his will, and to which the descendants of his sisters laid claim if he died intestate as to this property in the United States. The origin of this fund is full of interest. Kosciusko came here in 1776, entered our army as a volunteer in the Engineers, participated in all the struggles of our revolutionary war, and retired at its close with the rank of Brigadier General, poorer than when he came, and actually a creditor of our government for his military pay. During his absence in Europe, participating in the heroic struggle of his native land, he became entitled, under a military certificate, to the sum of $12,280.54, and not being able to receive it then, Congress passed a law in 1799 giving him interest from the 1st of January, 1793, to 31st December, 1797. When the money was paid it was invested in American stocks, and placed under the care of Jefferson. By judicious care and management the fund increased to the sum of $17,159.63, which was the subject of the suit in 1852. Before his departure from the country, in 1798, he made his will in his own handwriting, directing this fund to be laid out in the purchase of young negroes, who were to be *educated and emancipated.* In regard to this, he wrote to Jefferson, September 15th, 1817, as follows:

"We all grow old, and for that reason, my dear and respectable friend, I ask you, as you have full power to do, to arrange it in such a manner, that after the death of our worthy friend, Mr. Barnes, some one as honest as himself may take his place, so that I may receive the interest of my money punctually; of which money after my death, you know the fixed destination. As for the present, do what you think best."

As the will of 1816 revoked the two previous wills, the disposition of the fund became canceled.

But in the will of 1817, by the second clause, he provided : "Je léque tous mes effets, ma voiture, et mon cheval y comprise à Madame et à Monsieur Zavier Zeltner, les hommes ce dessus." It was on this clause the dispute arose; because it was claimed that by the words "mes effets," the property in the United States passed, that it was a residuary devise, and that all went to the two persons named. On the other hand, it was claimed, that as Kosciusko, having been domiciled for fifteen years in France, and was only temporarily sojourning in Switzerland, that the law of France should control, and that the proper interpretation of such a phrase was that it referred to property as belonging at the time and which was attached to his person, and that the subsequent words restricted its meaning, and prevented it having a general signification. It was held that as to this property in the United States Kosciusko died intestate; and that, on the principle that personal property, wherever it may be, is to be distributed, in case of intestacy, according to the law of the domicile of the intestate, that the disposition of this property should be governed by the law of France, the proper domicile of Kosciusko. There vas some difficulty to ascertain the domicile, but it was shown that he did not leave Poland compulsorily, which would be an important consideration in determining his *intent;* but he left voluntarily to obtain a civil status in France, which he conscientiously thought he could not enjoy in Poland whilst it continued under a foreign dominion.

With regard to real estate, a different rule prevails. It would not comport with the dignity or independence of one country to allow real property, which by its nature is fixed and immovable, to be controlled and affected by foreign laws. Hence it is the law of the place where the real estate is situated that governs in its distribution, and as to the proper execution of a will devising it. This is expressed by the formula that the *lex locus rei sitæ* governs. Thus, a devise of lands in England, though made abroad, must be executed pursuant to the English statute. Thus, where C made his will abroad, devising lands in England, but the same was executed in the presence of *two* witnesses, (three being necessary, at the time of its execution, to devise lands in England) in accordance with the law where he was domiciled, it was held that the will must be void as to lands in England, which lands can only pass by such a will as the laws of England require, and that the *lex rei sitæ* should govern.*

And if a testator, by his will, direct personal property to be invested; in another State, in certain trusts of real estate there lawful, but not lawful by the law of the State where the testator is domiciled, the trusts will be declared void.

This was the case where a testator, a resident of the State of New York at the time of his death, who, by his will, directed his personal property and the proceeds of his real estate there situated to be invested in real estate in the State of Ohio, upon trusts which were invalid by the law of New York, it was held that the devise in trust was invalid, as it was inconsistent with the law of the testator's domicile.†

Jarman‡ considers that a will of realty is construed according to the law of the country where the land is situated; but Story, § Greenleaf,‖ and others are of opinion that this doctrine of the *lex rei sitæ* does not apply to the construction, as distinguished from the execution, of wills. There are several American authorities on either side, the balance, however, being in favor of the law as stated by Jarman.

A will has always been presumed, in England, to

---

* Coppin v. Coppin, 2 P. Wms. 291. This was accepted as an indisputable proposition, in Lynes v. Townsend, 33 N. Y. 558.
† Wood v. Wood, 5 Paige, 596 ; 9 Wheat. 565.
‡ Vol. I, 1.
§ Conf. Laws, Sec. 479.
‖ Evid. 671.

speak only from the death of the testator as to personalty, but before 1838, from its date as to realty. By 1 Vict., Ch. 26, devises and bequests were to be from *death* of the testator, unless a contrary intention appears. The rules thus settled by this act have long been adopted in most of our States.* A will is presumed in the following States to speak only from the testator's death, as regards the subject-matter (as distinguished from the objects) of the testator's bounty: California, Maryland, Missouri, New York, and Pennsylvania.

In Virginia, wills of land speak from the making of the instrument, unless it discloses an intention to the contrary.† It is so in Massachusetts, New Hampshire, Vermont, Maine, Indiana, Illinois, North Carolina, Connecticut, and Kentucky; though a testator may, in these States, convey by his will any after-acquired land, provided he declares his intention to that effect. The construction, however, on these statutes virtually raises a presumption that wills speak only from the death of the testator, if there is nothing in the context to the contrary.‡

It seems the better opinion, that the law of the domicile of the testator will govern as to what shall be regarded as personal estate, and what real. Thus, in Kentucky, shares in the capital stock of railroad companies are considered as real property,§

* Gold v. Judson, 21 Conn. 616.
† 8 Cranch, 66; G. Stat. (Mass.) C. 92; 7 Met. 141; 6 N. H. 47.
‡ Cushing v. Aylwin, 12 Met. 169.
§ Washburne, Real Prop. I, 166.

and, according to this rule, a will made by a person domiciled there must be executed as a will of real estate, to convey such shares.

And the law of the place of domicile must govern as to what ought to be regarded as testamentary capacity.

Thus, in England, administration was granted upon the probate of the will of a married woman, domiciled in Spain, she being also a native of that country, it appearing that by the law of that country a *feme covert* may dispose of her property by will, with certain limitations, the same as a *feme sole*.*

* Re Maraver, 1 Hagg. 498.

CHAPTER VIII.

Construction of Wills.

It is obvious that within the scope of the present work it is inexpedient to treat of this subject extensively; it is considered only necessary to advert to a few of the leading and generally recognized rules followed in the construction of wills, both here and in England.

The main purpose, in this direction, is to ascertain the true intention of the testator, from the language used in the instrument, and this intention shall prevail above every other construction which might be placed on the language. This is the cardinal rule of all construction, but it is to be taken with this limitation, that the intention will govern only so far as it is consistent with the rules of law. The general intent overrides all mere technical and grammatical rules of construction.

This intention is to be ascertained from the whole will taken together, from a full view of everything contained within "the four corners of the instrument,"* and not from the language of any particular provision when taken by itself; and, for the purpose of construction, a will and codicil may be considered together, and construed as different parts

---

* Hoxie v. Hoxie, 7 Paige, 187.

of the same instrument.* But where several parts are absolutely irreconcilable, the latter must prevail.†

The rule as to intention, governing in all cases, is somewhat liable to misconception, because it is susceptible of, and may be taken in, two senses.

For by intention, it may be inferred that we are to seek for some probable purpose as existing in the testator's mind at the time; or may seek to extract that intention from the meaning of the language which he has used. It is in this latter sense alone in which construction is employed. The will must be in writing, and the only question is, what is the meaning of the words used in that writing? And to ascertain this, every part of it must be considered, with the help of those surrounding circumstances which are admissible in evidence to explain the words, and to put the court as nearly as possible in the situation of the writer.

This was well expressed in Cole v. Rawlinson, ‡ by Lord Holt when he said: "The intent of a testator will not do, unless there be sufficient words in the will to manifest that intent; neither is the intent to be collected from the circumstances of his estate, and other matters collateral and foreign to the will, but from the words and tenor of the will itself." The rule was well illustrated in the case of Doe v. Dring, § where a testator, intending, no doubt, to dispose of *all* his property for the benefit of his family, used these words: "All and singular

---

* Hone v. Van Schaick, 3 Barb. Ch. 488. ‡ 1 Salk. 234.
† 2 W. Bl. 976. § 2 Mau. and Sel. 454.

my *effects* of what nature and kind soever." Lord Ellenborough said, that if he were asked his private opinion as to what the testator really meant when he used these words, he would reply, that he must be supposed to have meant that which his duty prescribed to him, to convey *all* his property for the maintenance of his family; but as a *judge*, he was not at liberty to collect his meaning from matters *dehors*, but only from expressions used on the face of the will, and that the expression "effects" had always a meaning, in the absence of anything in the context, which necessarily excluded real estate. However, if the context shows that by the expression, "all my personal estates," the testator meant to include real property, it will be so held by reason of the clear intention manifested on the face of the will.*

An introductory clause expressing a testator's desire to dispose of all the property he should "leave behind him" may be referred to, to construe the will as passing all lands belonging to the testator at the time of his death.†

It is one of the most troublesome questions in law, as to how far parol evidence can be admitted to ascertain the intention of a testator. The principle was early established, that parol evidence should not be admitted to vary, contradict, or enlarge the terms of a will, and this is still rigidly adhered to. This was well established in what is

---

* Roe v. Pattison, 16 East. 221 ; Wheeler's Heirs v. Dunlap, 13 B. Mon. 293.
† Youngs v. Youngs, 45 N. Y. 254.

known as Lord Cheney's Case,* where it is said that "otherwise it were great inconvenience that not any may know by the written words of the will what construction to make, if it might be controlled by collateral averment, out of the will."

Chancellor Kent, in Mann v. Mann,† examined this subject with much industry and learning, and declared the result to be: that from Cheney's Case down to this day, it has been a well-settled rule that parol evidence cannot be admitted to supply or contradict, enlarge or vary the words of a will, nor to explain the intention of the testator, except in two specific cases: 1st. Where there is a latent ambiguity arising *dehors* the will, as to the person or subject meant to be described; and 2d. To rebut a resulting trust.

What is a latent ambiguity is thus described in the quaint but expressive language of Lord Bacon: "*Latens* is that which seemeth certain, and without ambiguity for anything that appeareth upon the deed or instrument; but there is some collateral matter out of the deed that breedeth the ambiguity; as, if I grant my manor of S to J F and his heirs, here appeareth no ambiguity at all; but if the truth be that I have the manors both of North S and South S, this ambiguity is matter in fact, and, therefore, it shall be holpen by averment, whether of them was that the party intend should pass."

A patent ambiguity is one that is apparent on the face of the will, and is only to be remedied by con-

---

* 5 Co. 68 b. † 1 Johns. Ch. 231.

struction of the language, if possible. As, for example, if the devise is to one of the sons of J S, who has several sons, such an uncertainty in the description of the devisee cannot be explained by parol proof.*

As a general rule, courts do not admit parol evidence in cases of patent ambiguity; but on this head there is a difference of decision in this country. We have no uniform rule throughout the United States, either by statute or construction, as to the extent to which parol testamentary evidence is admissible. In some States, the English rules will be followed in the main, which is to admit no extrinsic evidence except to explain a latent ambiguity. But in many of the States, undoubtedly, extrinsic evidence of the testator's circumstances, as distinguished from his intention, will be admitted in aid of the construction of any expression left ambiguous by the context.† In New York, the courts adhere to the English rule, and admit no extrinsic evidence, except to explain a latent ambiguity.‡ In Maryland, the strict rules of construction prevail, and no parol evidence is admitted except as in England. § The same is the rule in Ohio. ‖

It seems to be a universally received doctrine in the American courts, that extrinsic evidence of the

---

* 2 Vern. 624.

† Brownfield v. Brownfield, 20 Penn. 55; Johnson v. Johnson, 32 Ala. 637. Where there is no ambiguity on the face of a will, evidence is inadmissible to explain it: Hill v. Alford, 46 Ga. 247.

‡ Jackson v. Sill, 11 Johns. 201.

§ Walston v. White, 5 Md. 297.

‖ Worman v. Teagarden, 2 Ohio N. S. 380.

declarations of the testator, made at the time, before or after the execution of the will, cannot be received to show the intention of the testator by the use of particular words therein, or by its general scope; as, that by the use of the word "children" he meant to include step-children;* or that a bequest to the parent was intended for the children of such parent, who was known by the testator to have died; or that the term "children" was intended to include illegitimate children;† or in any sense to vary the express provisions of the will, or to show in what sense he used a well-settled term of law.‡ Nor are the declarations of the testator admissible to show the existence of a will at the time they were made.§ But, in a case in Michigan, it was held, where, after the death of the testator, a will twenty-five years old was discovered in a barrel among waste papers, and either torn or worn into several pieces, which were scattered loose among the papers in the barrel, that the declarations of the testator, made after the date of the will, were admissible, not as separate and independent evidence of revocation, but as tending to explain whether the instrument was thus torn accidentally, or with intent to revoke.‖ The code of California has settled this question for that State;

---

* Asay v. Hoover, 5 Penn. 21.
† 2 Sneed, 618.
‡ Allen v. Allen, 18 How. (U. S.) 385.
§ Betts v. Jackson, 6 Wend. 187.
‖ Lawyer v. Smith, 8 Mich. 411.

it excludes all declarations of the testator's intention.*

To ascertain the intention of the testator from the language of the instrument, certain rules of construction have been established, which have obtained the acquiescence and authority of the courts. If technical words are used by the testator, he will be presumed to have employed them in their legal sense, unless the context contain a clear indication to the contrary.† Courts, therefore, have no right or power to say that the testator did not understand the meaning of the words he has used, or to put a construction upon them different from what has been long received, or what is affixed to them by the law.‡ There can be no place for construction, for the discovery of the testator's intention, when he has used words of an unequivocal, definite sense in law, and, however it may frustrate any presumed worthy designs, the import of the terms as used must prevail.§

In Hicks v. Salitt,|| the court said: "When a testator uses a word which has a well-known, ordinary acceptation, it must appear very certain that he has said, on the face of the will, that he uses it in another sense, before the ordinary sense can be interfered with. . . . . In order to alter the meaning of a word, it must appear, not that the testator *might* have meant it in a different sense,

---

* Civil Code, 1340; Estate of Garraud, 35 Cal. 336.
† 4 Vesey, 329; 1 Salk. 233.
‡ Hodgson v. Ambrose, 1 Doug. 341.
§ Theall v. Theall, 6 La. 220.
|| 18 Jur. 915.

but that he *must* have meant it in a different sense."

The right of every testator to use words in a sense different from the technical legal sense, provided it is apparent, is well established and acknowledged. Thus, in deference to the context, the word "money" has been held to pass stock in the funds;* though its technical meaning, according to Coke, only implies gold and silver, or the lawful circulating medium of a country.†

This technical meaning of the word was applied in Mann v. Mann,‡ where a testator bequeathed "all the rest, residue, and remainder of the *moneys* belonging to his estate at the time of his decease," which was held not to comprehend promissory notes, bonds and mortgages, and other securities, there being nothing in the will itself to show that the testator intended to use the word in that extended sense. And the words "nephews and nieces" have been held to include great-nephews and great-nieces, different from the import of these terms as settled in law;§ and the word "family" has been held to include a husband.‖

In the case of Hussey v. Berkeley,¶ Lord Nottingham, upon the question whether the testatrix

---

* Dowson v. Gaskoin, 2 Kee. 14. The word "money" used in making a devise in a will, will be construed to include both personal and real property, if it appears from the context, and on the face of the instrument, that such was the intention of the testator. Estate of Miller, 48 Cal. 165.
† Co. Litt. 207.
‡ 1 Johns. Ch. 231.
§ James v. Smith, 14 Sim. 214.
‖ 5 Vesey, 159.
¶ 2 Eden, 194.

intended to include great-grandchildren under the term grandchildren, considered the fact that she had, in another part of the will, called a great-grandchild her granddaughter, as conclusive evidence of her intention to include such great-granddaughter in the residuary clause of the will, under the general description of her grandchildren.

The court is bound to give effect to every word of a will without change or rejection, provided an effect can be given to it not inconsistent with the general intent of the whole will taken together.* Thus, if one devises land to A B in fee, and afterwards in the same will devises the same land to C D, for life, both parts of the will shall stand; and in the construction of the law, the devise to C D shall be first.† But when it is impossible to form one consistent whole, the separate parts being *absolutely* irreconcilable, the latter will prevail.‡ Thus, where the testator, by one clause of his will, bequeathed a slave to his son, remainder to his issue, remainder over; and by a subsequent clause bequeathed the same slave to his daughter, with like limitations, it was held that the clauses were inconsistent, and the last revoking the first, that the daughter was entitled to the legacy.§

If a testator's intention cannot operate to its full

---

* Thus, in a case in California, Norris v. Henley, 27 Cal. 439, a testator devised his real estate upon a particular street, one-third to each of three persons by name, "to have and to hold their lifetime, and then to go to their heirs and assigns, *but never to sell.*" It was held to create a fee, and these words, "never to sell," had no effect.

† Cro. Eliz. 9.

‡ Sims v. Doughty, 5 Ves. 243 : Parks v. Parks, 9 Paige, 107.

§ Frazer v. Boone, 1 W. R. Hill, 367.

extent, it shall take effect as far as possible.* And where a will contains different trusts, some of which are valid, and others void or unauthorized by law; or where there are distinct and independent provisions as to different portions of the testator's property, or different estates or interests in the same portions of the property are created, some of which provisions, estates, or interests are valid, and others are invalid, the valid trusts, provisions, estates, or interests created by the will will be preserved, unless those which are valid and those which are invalid are so dependent upon each other that they cannot be separated without defeating the general intent of the testator.†

Words, in general, are to be taken in the ordinary and grammatical sense, unless a clear intention to to use them in another can be collected.‡ Thus, in Young v. Robertson,§ it is laid down: The primary duty of a court of construction, in the interpretation of wills, is to give to each word employed, if it can with propriety receive it, the natural ordinary meaning which it has in the vocabulary of ordinary life, and not to give words employed in that vocabulary an artificial, a secondary, and a technical meaning. Thus, a testator, in a clause of his will, provided that the share of the estate of any of his children dying without issue should be equally divided among the survivors of his children or

---

* 3 P. Wms. 259; Cal. Civ. Code, 1317.
† Parks v. Parks, 9 Paige, 107; Williams v. Williams, 4 Seld. 525; Hawley v. James, 16 Wend. 61.
‡ Chrystie v. Phyfe, 19 N. Y. 344.
§ 8 Jur. N. S. 825.

grandchildren, and it was held that a step-daughter was not a surviving *child* of the testator, within the intent and meaning of this clause of the will, so as to entitle her to a portion of the shares of one of the testator's daughters, who died without leaving issue, even though this step-daughter was acknowledged to be of the family, and treated there as a child.*

And the word "children" does not, ordinarily and properly speaking, comprehend grandchildren or issue generally; these being included in that term is only permitted in two cases, viz., from necessity which occurs where the will would remain inoperative unless the sense of the word "children" were extended beyond its natural import, and where the testator has clearly shown by *other* words that he did not intend to use the term "children" in its proper, actual meaning, but in a more extensive sense. In Osgood v. Lovering,† the word was held to include grandchildren, it being apparent from the context, that this was the meaning given by the testator.‡

This term imports legitimate children only;§ but if it is notorious that a testator had no such legitimate children, but had others who went by reputation, and were acknowledged as his children, these can take under this term.‖

In Lord Woodhouslee v. Dalrymple,¶ a legacy was

---

* Matter of Hallet, 8 Paige, 375.
† 33 Maine, 464.
‡ Hughes v. Hughes, 12 B. Mon. 121.
§ Metham v. Duke of Devon, 1 P. Wms. 529.
‖ Cartwright v. Vawdry, 5 Vesey, 530; Gardner v. Heyer, 2 Paige, 12.
¶ 2 Meriv. 419.

given "to the *children* of the late C K, who shall be living at my decease"; C K being dead at the date of the will leaving illegitimate children, (of whom three were living at the testator's death) and not having had at the date of the will, nor having ever had, any *legitimate* children, the three illegitimate children were held to be entitled.

The word "issue" is a term of more general signification than children; it includes not only children, but all lineal descendants, however remote, for successive generations. It has been called by Lord Holt a *nomen collectivum;*[*] but this word has frequently been construed to signify children, where it was so apparent from the context.[†]

The phrase, "dying without issue," in wills, for a long time occasioned much obscurity, and was a fruitful source of litigation. Thus, if an executory devise were limited to take effect on a dying without *heirs*, or on a failure of issue, or "without leaving issue," or "without *issue*," the limitation was held to be void, because the contingency was *too remote*, as these phrases being interpreted to mean an *indefinite failure of issue*, the vesting of the estate would thus be suspended beyond the period allowed by law. But other words used in the will might control this construction, as to show that the testator intended to limit the vesting of the estate to issue living at the time of the death of the first taker. This contrary intent would be inferred by the use of the words "living," or "leav-

---

[*] 1 Vent. 231; Moore v. Moore, 12 B. Mon. 655.
[†] Sibley v. Perry, 7 Ves. 522; Pope v. Pope, 14 Beav. 591.

ing issue behind," or "without children." Unless such qualifying words, however, were used, the words "*dying without issue*" were construed as meaning an indefinite failure of issue.*

The statute law of New York, and many of the States, has settled the construction of this term, as it is provided under these statutes that it shall be construed to mean *heirs* or *issue* living at the death of the person named as ancestor.†

Gifts and devises are sometimes made to a "family," and the decisions have given to the word the same construction as "kindred," or "relations." ‡

In Robinson v. Waddelon, § a testator gave all the residue of his effects to be equally divided between his two daughters and their husbands *and families;* the court rejected the words "husbands and families," and held that the two daughters took the residue equally and absolutely as tenants in common.

Roper has the following observations on devises and bequests to a *family:* "The word *family*, when applied to personal property, is synonymous with "kindred" or "relations." If it be asked, of what family is A, the question will be answered by being informed from what person he is descended, and whoever is related by blood to that stock is related to, and of, the family of A. This being the *ordinary* acceptation of the word, it may never-

---

* Hopkins v. Jones, 2 Barr, 69; Moore v. Moore, 12 B. Mon. 653.
† N. Y. Rev. Stat. Vol. III, p. 12.
‡ 9 Vesey, 319.
§ 8 Sim. 134.

theless be confined to particular relations by the context of wills; or the term may be enlarged by it, so that the expression may in some cases mean *children*, or *next of kin*, and in others may even include relations by marriage."*

Personal chattels are not unfrequently described by reference to locality, as where a testator bequeaths the "household goods," "things," "property," or "effects" which are in or about a house. These words, it seems, in general, will not pass cash, bank notes, bonds, notes, or other *choses in action* being in the house.†

In Woolcomb v. Woolcomb,‡ a testator bequeathed to his wife all his household goods, and other goods, plate, and stock, within doors and without, and bequeathed the residue of his estate to J S. It was held that the ready money and bonds did not pass by the word *goods*, for then the bequest of the residue would be void.

Bequests of "chattels and effects" are clearly adequate to pass the whole personal estate, yet where these words are collocated with household goods, they may be, and frequently are, restrained to articles *ejusdem generis*.§

A testator, after several legacies of bank stock and other stock and money, concluded his will as follows: "The remainder of my worldly substance, consisting

---

* Legacies, Ch. II, Sec. 10.
† Jones v. Sefton, 4 Vesey, 166.
‡ 3 P. Wms. 112.
§ Timewell v. Perkins, 2 Atk. 103. The word "estate" in a will carries everything, unless restrained by particular expressions: Turbett v. Turbett, 3 Yeates, 187.

of furniture, bedding, carpets, china, kitchen furniture, looking-glasses, crockery, etc., I give to my two daughters, etc.; these, with all money of mine that may remain in bank at the time of my death, with all claims or demands of whatever nature, I give to my two daughters, etc." The testator had several shares of bank stock and other stock, not specifically bequeathed. It was held that this bank stock and other stock did not pass under the above bequest.*

The courts of equity, even in England, do not seem disposed to apply the rule *ejusdem generis* with so much strictness as formerly. In the late case of Swinfen v. Swinfen,† it was decided that in a bequest particularized by one word, followed by general words, the latter was not to be restricted to things *ejusdem generis;* as where the bequest was, "all my estate at S or thereto adjoining, also all furniture, or other moveable goods here," it was held that the live-stock and implements of husbandry in and about the premises passed by the bequest. It was also held that money in the house at the time of the testator's death passed to the legatee.

In Brown v. Cogswell,‡ where the bequest was of "all my household furniture, wearing apparel, and all the rest and residue of personal property, saving and excepting one feather bed," it was held to carry the entire residuum of personal property. A bequest of furniture in a particular house (except plate) will include plated articles in use in the

---

* Delamater's Estate, 1 Wharton, 362.
† 20 Beav. 207.
‡ 5 Allen, 556.

house, the word "plate" meaning solid plate only. Such a bequest embraces only the articles permanently in use in the house.*

Words, however, in a will, which if allowed to stand would produce repugnant and inconsistent results, may be rejected.† Others may be supplied where there is no doubt in regard to the words intended, and others may be transposed and changed to carry out the sense and intention of the testator.‡

The will must be most favorably and benignly expounded to pursue and effectuate, if possible, the intention of the testator,§ and of two modes of construction, that is to be preferred which will prevent a total intestacy.‖ The strict rules of construction adopted in England, when strictly and unflinchingly applied, had often the effect of invalidating wills; but there has, of late, been evinced a tendency to relax this stringency of construction, and the proportion of wills and bequests which have been declared void for uncertainty has been constantly diminishing; and, at present, it is becoming more rare, unless through some fatal accident or miscarriage in the preparation of the instrument. The same tendency is observable in the decisions of the American courts.

Construction with the aid of precedents and anal-

---

* Holder v. Ramsbottom, 9 Jur. N. S. 350; Nichols v. Osborn, 2 P. Wms. 419.

† Pond v. Bergh, 10 Paige, 140 ; 12 Mass. 537; Estate of Wood, 36 Cal. 75.

‡ Wootton v. Redd, 12 Gratt. 196.

§ 3 Burr, 1634.

‖ 4 Vesey, 406.

ogies is only resorted to to ascertain the intention of a testator; all construction is subordinate to that single purpose; and analogy and precedent should have no further influence when they lead one side of the intention. They should only be used as our assistants to this end.

It will be found useful and appropriate, at the conclusion of this chapter, to give the seven propositions of Sir James Wigram, in his approved and reliable work respecting the admission of extrinsic evidence in aid of the interpretation of wills. He divided the subject into seven propositions, as follows:

Proposition I.—A testator is always presumed to use the words in which he expresses himself according to their strict and primary acceptation, unless from the context of the will it appears that he has used them in a different sense, in which case the sense in which he thus appears to have used them will be the sense in which they are to be construed.

Proposition II.—Where there is nothing in the context of a will from which it is apparent that a testator has used the words in which he has expressed himself in any other than their strict and primary sense, and where his words, so interpreted, are *sensible with reference to extrinsic circumstances*, it is an inflexible rule of construction, that the words of the will shall be interpreted in their strict and primary sense, and in no other, although they may be capable of some popular or secondary interpretation, and although the most conclusive evidence of intention to use them in such popular or secondary sense be tendered.

Proposition III.—Where there is nothing in the context of a will from which it is apparent that a testator has used the words in which he has expressed himself in any other than their strict and primary sense, but his words, so interpreted, are *insensible with reference to extrinsic circumstances*, a court of law may look into the extrinsic circumstances of the case, to see whether the meaning of the words be sensible in any popular or secondary sense, of which, *with reference to these circumstances*, they are capable.

Proposition IV.—Where the characters in which a will is written are difficult to be deciphered, or the language of the will is not understood by the court, the evidence of persons skilled in deciphering writing, or who understand the language in which the will is written, is admissible to *declare* what the characters are, or to inform the court of the proper meaning of the words.

Proposition V.—For the purpose of determining the object of a testator's bounty, or the subject of disposition, or the quantity of interest intended to be given by his will, a court may inquire into every *material* fact relating to the person who claims to be interested under the will, and to the property which is claimed as the subject of disposition, and to the circumstances of the testator, and of his family and affairs, for the purpose of enabling the court to identify the person or thing intended by the testator, or to determine the quantity of interest he has given by his will. The same (it is conceived) is true of every other disputed point, respecting which it can be shown that a knowledge of extrinsic facts can, in any way, be made ancillary to the right interpretation of a testator's words.

Proposition VI.—Where the words of a will, aided by evidence of the material facts of the case, are insufficient to determine the testator's meaning, no evidence will be admissible to prove what the testator intended, and the will (*except in certain special cases in Proposition VII*) will be void for uncertainty.

Proposition VII.—Notwithstanding the rule of law which makes a will void for uncertainty where the words, aided by evidence of the material facts of the case, are insufficient to determine the testator's meaning, courts of law, in certain special cases, admit extrinsic evidence of *intention*, to make certain the *person* or *thing* intended, where the description in the will is insufficient for the purpose. These cases may be thus defined : Where the object of a testator's bounty, or the subject of disposition, (*i. e.*, the *person* or *thing* intended) is described in terms which are applicable indifferently to more than one *person* or *thing*, evidence is admissible to prove which of the persons or things so described was intended by the testator.

INDEX.

A.

Abatement—of legacies, p. 96.
Accumulation—how far allowed in common law, p. 143.
    extraordinary case of, p. 143.
    limits to, p. 145.
Acknowledgment—of signature to will, p. 55.
Ademption—of legacy, p. 97.
Age—of person making will, pp. 68, 69.
    manner of reckoning, p. 69.
    extreme, not an incapacity, pp. 86, 87.
Alienation—suspension of power in will, how limited, p. 146.
    utmost period permitted, p. 147.
Alfred, King—will of, pp. 32, 33.
Ambiguity—latent, definition of, p. 188.
    latent, parol evidence admitted to explain, p. 188.
    patent, what it is, p. 188.
Animals—singular regard for in wills, pp. 77, 78.
    regard of Louis Bonard for, p. 82.
Annuity in will—when to commence, p. 117.
Attestation—of will, p. 64.
    forms of, p. 67.

B.

Bacon, Lord—maxim of, in regard to parol evidence, p. 129.
Bastard—not classed in law as a child, p. 124.
Bequest—meaning of, p. 93.
Blind persons—their capacity to make will, p. 70.

Bonard, Louis—will of, p. 82.
> singular life and belief of, pp. 81–83.

Bradford, Surrogate—his principles in admitting will of aged persons, p. 88.

Brinckerhoff, Dorothea—will of, p. 62.

Burial—directions for, in will, pp. 10, 16, 21, 77.

Burning will—a mode of revocation, p. 163.

C.

Cancelation of will—a mode of revocation, p. 163.
> what shall amount to, p. 169.

Canute—will of, p. 32.

Capacity—to make will, as to age, pp. 68, 85.
> physical and mental, pp. 69–71.

Charitable uses—devises to, formerly allowed, pp. 132, 133.
> doctrine of, derived from civil law, p. 133.
> doctrine of, existed in common law, pp. 135, 141.
> this denied in Levy v. Levy, p. 139.
> law of, has varied in New York, p. 135.
> researches of Prof. Dwight on, p. 151.
> what are, p. 133.

"Chattels and effects"—what shall pass by in will, p. 198.

Child—does not include step-child, p. 195.
> illegitimate, when a bequest to is good, p. 124.
> in *ventre sa mere* can take interest in will, p. 121.

Children—meaning of term in will, pp. 121, 122, 195.
> imports legitimate only, p. 195.

Clergy—early connection of with wills, p. 33.
> exclusive jurisdiction over wills, p. 35.
> intervention in probate matters, p. 34.
> their influence over the dying, pp. 36, 131.

Codicil—how far will control provision in will, p. 161.
> when it will cancel a will, p. 162.
> how several are to be construed, p. 160.

Concanen, Edward—will of, p. 111.

Conditions—in will, how far legal, p. 107.
> illegal, p. 113.
> precedent and subsequent, what are, pp. 103, 104.

Construction—of will, purpose of, pp. 185, 191.
Constantinople—bequest to poor of, p. 86.
Corporations—prohibited from taking by devise, p. 132.
>what are allowed to take by devise in New York, p. 142.
Coverture—formerly incapacitated woman making will, p. 90.
>not now generally an incapacity, p. 91.
Cromwell—singular bequest to, p. 18.
Cruger, Harriet Douglas—will of, p. 84.
>her history and singular delusion, p. 85.
Curtesy—married woman cannot defeat right in will in some States, p. 92.
>married women may defeat in New York, p. 92.
Cutting—a will equivalent to tearing, p. 164.

D.

Deaf and dumb—their capacity to make will, pp. 69, 70.
Declarations—of testator, not admitted to show intention in a will, p. 190.
Delusion—what it is, pp. 72, 75.
>of Harriet Douglas Cruger, p. 85.
Denbigh, Earl of—singular bequest to, p. 17.
Devise—meaning of term, distinguished from legacy, p. 93.
Domicile—how determined, p. 175.
>law of relating to wills part of leges gentium, p. 173.
>law of governs in interpretation of wills, p. 175.
>law of at time of decease governs, p. 176.
Drunken men—when incapable of making will, p. 71.

E.

Eccentricity—difference between and monomania, p. 76.
>remarkable case of, p. 76.
Ecclesiastical—jurisdiction over wills, rise of, p. 35.
>courts' decisions binding in law of wills, p. 40.
"Effects"—meaning of in will, pp. 187, 198.
>meaning of in will of Kosciusko, p. 179.

Emptor familiæ—position of in Roman law, p. 31.
Erasures—and interlineations in a will, effect of, p. 169.
Executor—appointment of in will, p. 52.
    allowed a year to settle estate, p. 114.
    duty of in paying legacy to child, p. 118.
    not disqualified to receive legacy, p. 120.
    responsibility of in paying legacies, p. 114.
    when to pay legacy, pp. 114, 115.

F.

"Family"—construction of term in will, pp. 192, 197.
    explanation of term by Roper, p. 197.
Female—able to make will earlier than male in some States, p. 69.
Females—their fondness for animals, p. 77.
Fraud—preventing revocation of a will, pp. 166, 168.
Funeral expenses—provided for in will, pp. 11, 14.
    directions for payment not necessary, p. 51.

G.

Geigley, William—will of, p. 108.
Grandchildren, construction of term in will, p. 193.
Greenwood, singular delusion of, p. 73.

H.

Harcourt, Mr. Granville—will of, p. 13.
Hœres—of Roman law, description of, p. 30.
Henry VIII—will of, providing for dean and canons of Windsor, p. 24.
Hindoos—no will among, p. 31.
Holographic will, p. 50.
    singular example of in California, p. 50.
Hunt, Benjamin F.—will of, illustrating law of domicile, p. 176.

I.

Insanity—definition of, p. 72.
    partial not recognized in early law, p. 73.
    partial, how far invalidates a will, p. 74.
Interest—on legacies, when to commence, p. 116.
    on specific legacies, p. 117.
    on legacy before payment causes legacy to vest, p. 100.
In terrorem—doctrine of, pp. 111, 112.
In extremis—persons in allowed to make nuncupative wills, p. 43.
    persons in frequently unduly influenced, p. 135.
Intention—governs in the construction of a will, pp. 95, 101, 185.
    most considered in revocation of will, p. 168.
    governs so far as consistent with rules of law, p. 185.
    how ascertained, p. 185.
    to operate as far as possible, if not wholly, p. 193.
"Issue"—meaning of term in a will, p. 196.
"Issue, dying without"—former construction of, p. 196.
    meaning now by statute, p. 197.

J.

Jefferson—farm of, at Monticello, devised by Commodore Levy, p. 106.
    given charge of fund belonging to Kosciusko, p. 179.
Justinian—law of as to portion reserved for children, p. 32.
    limited bishop's interference in probate matters, p. 34.
    limited military testament to those actually on an expedition, p. 48.

K.

Kensett, William—singular disposition of his body, p. 77.
Kerr, Catharine—will of, p. 58.
Kidd, Captain—treasures of, superstition regarding, p. 79.

Kosciusko—will of before United States Supreme Court, p. 178.
    interesting facts regarding his career, p. 179

L.

Latent ambiguity—what is, p. 188.
Legacy—abatement of, p. 96.
    ademption of, when takes place, p. 97.
    contingent, definition of, p. 97.
    conditional, and variety, pp. 103–105.
    conditional, what conditions are valid, p. 103.
    conditional, in restraint of marriage, p. 107.
    general, examples of, pp. 93–95.
    general, importance of distinction, p. 96.
    in lieu of dower draws interest from death of testator, p. 117.
    interest on, when to begin, pp. 116, 117.
    payable out of real estate, pp. 100, 102.
    payment of, pp. 114, 115.
    payment of, to whom, p. 118.
    pecuniary sometimes held specific, p. 95.
    specific, definition of, p. 93.
    specific, various examples of, p. 94.
    to infants, to whom paid, p. 118.
    to a class, who shall take, p. 122.
    vested, when becomes, pp. 99, 100.
Legatee—how ascertained in some cases, p. 125.
    error in description of, how remedied, p. 126.
    who may be, p. 119.
Levy, Commodore—remarkable will of, p. 136.
Lex domicilii—governs will of personal property, p. 174.
Lex rei sitæ—governs will of real property.

M.

Marriage—revokes will previously made by a woman, p. 157.
    of children, attempt to control, p. 113.

Marriage—*Continued.*
    restraint of, how far legal, p. 111.
    of poor maids, provisions of Henry Raine for, pp. 133, 134.

Married women—capacity to take legacy or devise, p. 119.
    legacy to, formerly paid to husband, p. 119.
    power of to make will of personal property, p. 91.
    law of American States is giving more enlarged privileges to, p. 91.
    power of, by will in New York, p. 92.

Masses—legacy to say, pp. 21, 25.

May, Thomas—singular bequest to, p. 17.

"Money"—strict meaning of, in a will, p. 192.
    may include stock in funds, p. 192.
    held to include real and personal property, p. 192.

Monticello—devised by Commodore Levy, p. 136.

Monomania—what it is, recognition of in law, p. 73.
    when will avoid will, p. 75.
    rise of theory in Dew v. Clark, p. 74
    different from eccentricity, p. 76.

N.

Nephews and nieces—who are meant by, p. 192.

Non compos mentis—incapacity of to make will, p. 71.
    who are, p. 72.

Nuncupative will—its nature, p. 42.
    limitations of in Statute of Frauds, p. 43.
    generally limited to soldiers, sailors, and persons in extremis, p. 43.
    decision on in Cole v. Mordaunt, p. 44.
    cases on numerous, since civil war, p. 49.
    opinion of Kent in relation to, p. 45.
    was in general use before Statute of Frauds, p. 42.
    how limited in New York and California, p. 48.
    limitations of, by statute in England, p. 48.

O.

Ordinary—his privileges in early English law, p. 37.

P.

Parol evidence—when admissible, pp. 123, 126, 129, 160.
    of contents of lost will is received, p. 160.
    is not so readily in England, p. 161.
    not admitted to vary, contradict, or enlarge the terms of a will, p. 187.
    in what cases is admitted, p. 188.
Pembroke, Earl of—curious will of, p. 15.
Perpetuities—statute against, p. 150.
Personal estate—when a bequest of may be specific, p. 97.
    may include real estate sometimes, p. 87.
Personal property—age at which will of may be made, p. 68.
"Personalty"—meaning of term in will, p. 120.
    law of domicile governs in wills, p. 173.
"Plate"—meaning of term in will, p. 200.
Power—execution of, in a will, p. 52.
Power of appointment—given married women to make will, pp. 52, 91.
Publication of will—and in what States required, pp. 60–64.

R

Raine, Henry—will of, p. 132.
Rationabiles partes—meaning of in early English law, p. 36.
Reading, Mrs. Kitty Jenkyn Packe—will of, p. 11.
Real estate—legacy payable out of, rule as to, p. 100.
    will of, pp. 38, 69.
Restraint of marriage—in will, p. 107.
    curious case of, p. 113.
    not permitted in Roman law, p. 107.

Restraint of marriage—*Continued.*
>of widow allowed in our law, p. 110.
>of widower not allowed, p. 111.
>in general not permitted, p. 113.

Revocation of will—may take place in two modes, p. 152.
>an implied revocation a subject of discussion, p. 153.
>by marriage of feme sole, p. 153.
>implied not by birth of child, p. 153.
>by marriage and birth of child implied, p. 154.
>by subsequent will, when, pp. 159, 162.
>not effected by writing "obsolete" on will, p. 162.
>by burning, canceling, tearing, etc., p. 163.
>what acts amount to in New York, p. 165.
>requires two things—act and intent, p. 166.

Ridley, Hon. Araminta Monck—will of, p. 106.
Robbins, James—will of, p. 110.
Roman will—nature, and manner of making, p. 32.
Roman Catholic—not to marry a, a condition in will, pp. 106, 111.
Roosevelt—will of, founding hospital in New York, p. 149.
Rose—will of declared void, founding "Rose Benevolent Institution," p. 150.

S.

Salisbury, Earl of—singular bequest to, p. 17.
Sandwich, Countess Dowager—will of, p. 11.
Scotchman—not to marry a, a condition in a will, p. 106.
Seal—not required in will, except in New Hampshire, p. 52
Seastedt, Eliza—will of, p. 63.
Senile dementia—what it is, p. 86.
>when an incapacity to make will, p. 87.

"Servants"—meaning of term in a will, p. 125.
Shakspeare—will of, p. 21.
>his singular provision for his wife, p. 22.

Signature—to will, effect of tearing off by a testator, p. 170.
Society for Prevention of Cruelty to Animals—bequest to, p. 82.

Solon—laws of relating to wills, p. 31
Specific legacy—defined, p. 93.
    interest on begins from testator's death, p. 116.
Starkey, John—will of, p. 14.
Statute—of Distributions, p. 37.
    of Frauds, pp. 38, 44, 53.
    of Frauds, influence of in jurisprudence, p. 38.
    of Mortmain, pp. 132, 135.
    of Wills, p. 38.
    of 43 Elizabeth in regard to charitable uses, p. 133.
    of 43 Elizabeth not in force in New York, p. 135.
    of 43 Elizabeth, where in force, p. 141.
Subscription—to will, p. 55.
Succession, universal—among Romans, p. 30.
Superstitious use—definition of, pp. 132, 133.
Surrogate—derivation of term, p. 40.

T.

Testament—meaning of term, p. 41.
Testamentary capacity—generally exists, p. 68.
    as to age, p. 68.
Testamentary disposition—law places limits on, pp. 130, 142.
    limits to, in early English law, p. 36.
Thelusson, Peter—extraordinary will of, p. 143.
Thompson, Mr.—singular habits of, p. 78.
Tonnele, John—will of, p. 56.
Trusts—what are valid in a will, p. 140.
Turner, Sharon—will of, p. 12.

U.

United States—bequests to, pp. 136, 140, 150.
Uses and trusts—law of, to avoid Statute of Mortmain, p. 132.

V.

Van Hanrigh, Mrs.—will of, p. 14.
Virginia—bequest to, in trust, by Commodore Levy, p. 133.

W.

West, Lady Alice—curious will of, p. 18.
Wife—who will answer for in a will, p. 124.
    reproachful allusions to in a will, pp. 11, 12.
    affectionate allusions to in a will, pp. 13, 14.
Will—acknowledgment of signature to, p. 55.
    appointment of executor in, p. 52.
    attestation of, p. 64.
    definition and nature of, p. 41.
    destroying, what it signifies, p. 164.
    directions in as to burial, pp. 10, 11, 16, 77
    directions in as to debts, p. 51.
    divided into two classes, verbal and written, p. 42
    duplicate, effect of destroying, p. 163.
    erasures in, p. 163.
    holographic, and where valid, p. 50.
    importance of, p. 9.
    inofficious, pp. 31, 75.
    introductory clause in, p. 51.
    language of, immaterial, p. 53.
    making, solemnity of act, pp. 9, 51.
    may consist of many instruments, pp. 52, 158.
    mode of writing, p. 53.
    nature of, among Romans, pp. 31, 32.
    not of effect until death, pp. 121, 152.
    opinions of others in, freely expressed, pp. 10, 15.
    of personal property, pp. 68, 121.
    of real estate, p. 69.
    of real estate, must conform to law where real estate is situated, p. 182.
    power of disposition by, in early law, p. 36.

Will—*Continued.*
    publication of, where required, pp. 60–64.
    qualities of, p. 152.
    references to wives in, pp. 11, 12, 110.
    restraints on marriage in, pp. 14, 105–108, 111.
    requisites as to execution of, p. 55.
    right to make did not exist in early society, p. 30.
    seal not required in, p. 52.
    signing of, how under Statute of Frauds, p. 54.
    signing of, illustrated in cases, pp. 56, 60.
    what it is necessary to contain, pp. 50, 51.
    witnesses to, number required, p. 64.

Widow—prohibited remarrying by will, p. 108.
    recommended to marry, p. 13.

Widower—cannot be prohibited remarrying by will, p. 110.

Witnesses—manner of signing by, pp. 64–66.
    number required in different States, p. 64.
    cannot take interest by the will, p. 119.
    cutting out names of in will, effect of, p. 164.

Z.

Zimmerman—will of, p, 10

www.ingramcontent.com/pod-product-compliance
Lightning Source LLC
Chambersburg PA
CBHW031831230426
43669CB00009B/1300